# GarbageOut

Get Serious About Living Your Life

# P. ASHWORTH

Horizon Publishing

GarbageOut Books may be purchased for educational, business or sales promotional use. For information, please send request to: contact@garbageoutdaily.com

FIRST EDITION

ISBN: 978-0-9973402-1-1

1. Personal development. 2. Professional development.
3. Self-help. 4. Motivational. 5. Empowerment. 6. Women-
  Personal Growth

Each day you have the opportunity to add something
beautiful to the moment—to your story

*~P. Ashworth*

# CONTENTS

## CHAPTER FOUR
## RECYCLE THE LESSON

## CHAPTER FIVE
## FREE UP SPACE TO GROW

GarbageOut

# INTRODUCTION

Life is About Movement
Learning, Growing, Changing and Transforming

*~P. Ashworth*

In life you have a choice to be trapped beyond movement or free as a bird. You have the power to remove any obstacle that gets in your way, but sometimes you can allow your power to be drained by the stresses of life. Life's setbacks, disappointments and failures can rob you of your will to move, to learn, to grow, to change, to transform; it's time to regain your strength and take back your power.

Find out what happens when you take a chance on you—put time and energy into discovering just how great you are. Be determined not to let your life be about regrets, sorrows or excuses. Make the decision to free yourself of whatever is holding you down, be determined to rise to your true worth. Open yourself up to your truth, your life, to happiness, to the many possibilities of life.

In these pages you will discover how to face the challenges that are holding you back. You may have doubts about taking a different path in life. Perhaps the thought of failure paralyzes you. *GarbageOut* will help you sift through your life and identify the garbage that keeps piling up and along the way guide you to finally let go.

*Be mindful of your thoughts.* Your mind reacts or responds to the thoughts that you allow to exist. The stories you tell yourself and the things you believe can either strengthen your resolve to live your truth or settle—give up on life. Seek to find answers that reveal who you truly are. As you get closer to discovering your true story, your unique gift and talents, you will find that life will challenge you, test your strength and dare you to move beyond your comfort zone; dare you to go to the next level, to be free.

When facing resistance while trying to accomplish your goals, thoughts will arise pressuring you to giving up. In that moment your mind is being flooded with self-defeating thoughts that produce fear, doubt and insecurity these thoughts can paralyze you from going any further. The key is to have a routine in place to help you push through negative feelings and come out on the other side.

On the onset self-defeating thoughts will be very strong causing internal turmoil, as you open each door you are removing the mental garbage that has accumulated over the years. You are now making room for the new you to surface, the courageous, bold, fearless—you.

Self-defeating thinking can be very much like garbage, cluttering your mind with thoughts that can suffocate the very life out of you. Negative thoughts will not just go away, you have to choose thoughts that will energize you, empower you and inspire you to live a life full of meaning and purpose. Be selective about the thoughts you allow to take up your mental space. It's important to understand that your mental state controls your emotional state giving power to thoughts that dictate your behavior, whether you are going to cower in fear or stand up fearlessly and live your life on your terms. The choice is up to you.

*GarbageOut* will motivate you to let go and keep only what will serve a purpose—make you better. *GarbageOut* is like having your own personal therapist, coach and confidant with you at all times. There are questions and insights that will encourage you to take an honest look at your life. The answers you give will help you to uncover your hidden story—your truth.

Each chapter is fill with journal entries that stress the importance of being in control, being aware of your thoughts and how they affect every aspect of your life.

Bookmark your favorite entries so you can go back and read them as often as you like, to keep you inspired along your journey. You will be motivated to start thinking and responding in a way that will keep the garbage from piling up in your life; opening the way for you to experience life in a whole new light.

My hope is that "GarbageOut" inspires you to learn more about yourself, to grow, to change and to transform. Change can be the best thing that ever happen to you; in this moment make the decision to remove the garbage from your life, to live a courageous, bold and fearless life, to be confident and at peace with who you are. It's time to clean house and get serious about living your life!

# CHAPTER ONE

## "GarbageOut"
## LET IT GO

## DUMP IT AND LEAVE IT

Letting go is not always easy, but it is necessary. Just imagine if you never threw away your garbage, allowing it to pile up in your home day after day, week after week, month after month, year after year—the conditions would be so unbearable that it would be impossible to move, let alone think. Your home would be a health hazard. The odor would overtake you. This is exactly what happens when you accumulate mental garbage—the fear, the doubt, and the insecurity are like odors that begin to surface in your day to day life. Anger, frustration, depression, confusion, guilt, weight gain, health problems, and financial problems start to build, and your attitude can start to stink. Mental garbage can be seen in your speech, behavior and in the action you choose to take or not to take.

Everyone throws away at least one piece of garbage daily. The garbage is dropped in the garbage can and you don't think twice about it. Most of you have heard the phrase, "she's carrying a lot of baggage." Carrying around garbage is worse.

*The mental garbage you carry is not only heavy but, it literally builds up inside of you; it is toxic*

Having a routine to throw away your garbage is necessary. When you put your garbage out on the curb for the garbage man to pick up, you don't run after the truck to get it back, if anything you may run after the garbage truck because you forgot a bag of garbage that needed to be thrown away.

This is how you should view the garbage that fills your mind, throw it away and forget about it. With every experience you encounter, you can choose to take the garbage away with you—the pain, the hurt, the regret, the fear, the insecurity or you can choose to dump it and leave it. Which will you choose? You have to be able to filter through your life experiences, keep what will be useful in your journey and leave the rest. Some people take their physical garbage out everyday, others once a week. The point is—it's done routinely.

If you do not have a routine to mentally de-clutter your mind, the garbage will continue to invade your mental space and take control of your life. The garbage will stop you from growing as a person, essentially affecting every part of your life—your actions, thoughts and emotions. You will go through the motions of living, but you will not be living at all.

Life will seem directionless, without meaning or purpose. Your vision will become blurred from carrying around childhood disappointments, stress from work and family, burdens of past mistakes and failures, your friend's garbage and the perceptions other people try to project onto you. Everything from your past, present and future will be trying to co-exist. All the pain, sadness and grief would constantly tell you what you can't do.

*The cloud must be lifted; you are affecting your*
*Present state and your future*

It is time for a new beginning, it is time to claim your joy and claim your life; it is time to throw out the garbage that is infiltrating your mind and causing fear, doubt and insecurity to rule your life. Replace it with rejuvenating thoughts that will produce a brand new attitude leading you to a fresh new place of courage, boldness and fearlessness.

When you hold onto thoughts that seek to defeat you, you become weighed down feeling as if your very soul has been taken away from you. These thoughts leave you functioning in a robotic state. There seems to be no meaning in your life, you feel as if you are dying on the inside. The garbage—fear, insecurity and doubt takes control of your life—producing stress and anxiety, preventing you from moving or thinking because a barrier has emerged between you and your success. It is time to let go. Whether your goal is to start your own business, make a career change, lose weight, improve relationships, be debt free, create work life balance, write a book, discover your talents or gift. The first step is to remove the garbage, to remove the clutter would be a nicer way to say it, but sometimes it's much deeper, requiring you to get tough with yourself. Clean house and refuse to hold onto or accumulate any more garbage in your life. Position yourself to be mindful about what's going on in your life both mentally and physically.

*When you are mindful you do not make room for nonsense, you do not make room for thoughts that cloud your vision and cause unnecessary distractions*

Being mindful puts you in a state of awareness. When the unexpected happens you are able to take the necessary steps and take care of your business, your life is your business. If you need to rearrange something so be it, if you need to take time for yourself, take it. If you are not able to get away just take a moment, breathe, go for a walk, be still and pray. The mental garbage that you hold onto fear, doubt, insecurity and another people's perceptions create confusion and turmoil within. When it comes to your personal and professional growth you cannot hold onto thoughts that block your path—your life. When you make the decision to let go of thoughts that add no value to your life you are freeing up space to grow.

*You have to get to a place where you are clear about who you are, where you are in life, where you are going and confidently take intentional steps to get there*

**BE HONEST WITH YOURSELF, LET GO AND SOAR**

## INSIDE VIEW

Before you can create the life you want on the outside, you must first create a calm, peaceful and cohesive environment on the inside. Every idea, goal and dream starts in your mind. Whether they survive is totally up to you. When you create balance and control mentally, you empower yourself to:

- Stay focused despite unexpected crises

- Listen objectively to others

- Rebound quickly from mistakes

- Make effective decisions

- Be stimulated rather than discouraged from challenges

- Achieve goals regardless of any setbacks

- Stay on track to accomplish your goals

Obstacles are going to surface in life. The key is to overcome them and keep it moving. Overcoming obstacles strengthens you for the journey that lies ahead.

There will be situations in life that have the potential to negatively affect you; if you allow the negative thoughts to win, your internal garbage begins to build. You become loaded down unable to move in any direction. Now in the present moment, you are dealing with the issues of the past as well as issues resulting from your current situation. This is where garbage begins to accumulate, continuing to compound into your future. You have to come to a point where you say, "Enough is Enough" and take the steps necessary to remove the garbage and keep it out.

As you learn how to process and balance the things that are going on in your life, you will begin to gain control over your thinking and positive action will follow as you begin to take intentional steps to remain in control. Your thoughts will always precede your action so that's where the work must begin. Learn to face past issues that have a hold on you and let them go. The past cannot be relived, but you have your whole life ahead of you—this is where your focus should lie. Live in the present, the present is now, decide now to stop allowing your past, negative thoughts, people and situations to control you. Talk your way through it, get support and take one step at a time. When you become mentally grounded basically, three things start to happen:

1. You become focused

2. You become determined

3. You become unstoppable

This does not mean that you will not experience disappointments, setbacks or even make mistakes, it means that you will quickly rebound from difficult situations and not allow the mental garbage to build up, disrupt your thinking or your life, you will remain focused. Right away you will know what to do with garbage when it shows up in your life, throw it away—translated, *dump it and leave it,* be determined to succeed and do not allow anything or anyone to get in your way. Developing a no nonsense attitude that does not tolerate any garbage removes internal barriers making you unstoppable.

**EVERYDAY REPEAT**

I am focused, I am determined, I am unstoppable

**ANYTHING THAT DOES NOT SERVE A PURPOSE HAS NO PLACE IN YOUR LIFE**

# GARBAGEOUT

When you commit to throwing away fear, doubt and insecurity; you make room for courage to surface, boldness to emerge and fearlessness to take control. You put yourself in a position to be happy and to succeed in both your personal and professional life.

Once you choose to change the inside view of your life, your outside view will change. You will transform the very being of who you are, your reality will not be the same. Your confidence will begin to shine through. A bold new attitude will surface and fear will not hold you back.

Living your best life starts from the inside. Be mindful of how you think, decisions you make and how you respond to life. Your thoughts are the beginning of your story. The first step to finding your true story is to remove the garbage. Let go and free up space, so you can begin to discover just how great you are!

*The truth is we all are living a story*
*The question is are you living your true story*

## TAKE ACTION DESPITE YOUR INSECURITIES

Make your desire greater than your insecurities. Many people are insecure about their talent, knowledge or skill level to get the job done. It's normal for unfamiliar things to cause you to feel insecure. The goal is to change the way you view yourself and your journey. Changing the way you view all the hurdles you may have to jump or the fall you may experience, may seem a little scary but it is worth it. It will take perseverance, but the work will pay off, giving you that extra momentum to build up your strength for the journey ahead. Each hurdle you jump will boost your confidence in your abilities and decrease anxiety. It will get to a point where your insecurities will no longer be a factor in your decision making because you have come to understand that you can develop your talents, increase your knowledge and improve your skills along the way. When you throw away your insecurities you are embracing your power.

*Take one hurdle at a time—just keep up the pace. With every hurdle you jump, you are throwing away garbage that says, "You can't make that jump." Respond by saying, "Bam! In your face, watch me."*

Insecurities can be conquered, with each step outside your comfort zone—your confidence will grow. Be persistent and intentional in your actions. The peace from within will begin to emerge and more importantly, you will begin to discover just how strong you are. Learning to dismiss self-defeating thoughts when they arise and throwing them out of your mind before they overwhelm you is the key to managing mental garbage and overcoming your insecurities. Your thoughts can either fuel feelings of inadequacy or help you overcome them. You are who you believe you are; believe that you are powerful, believe that you are worthy, believe that you are somebody, believe that you are unstoppable, believe that you can accomplish anything you set your mind to, then turn your beliefs into action!

When thoughts that cause you to feel insecure emerge, ask yourself, "Will these thoughts hinder me or help me move forward?" If a thought is hindering you from moving forward, then it has to go in the garbage pile. If a thought is encouraging action that will help you move forward with your life, then you know that you are taking steps in the right direction. Feeling of insecurity will arise; you have to prove who is in control. When you stand up for yourself the voice of insecurity will take a back seat and the volume will get lower and lower because your attention has shifted from the thought pattern of what you can't do, to what you can do. During this process you are building your self-esteem and taking notice of your power—you are building awareness that will put you on the path to discovering your greatness!

What insecurities are you holding onto?

_____

_____

_____

_____

_____

_____

_____

What steps are you going to take to let go of your insecurities?

_____

_____

_____

_____

_____

_____

_____

Pay attention to when you feel confident and secure

## THE SEED OF DOUBT

When rejection happens or you are in an unfamiliar space, you may want to crawl under a rock and hide. This is where doubt tries to sneak in, but there is no time for hiding. Look at the reasons why you were rejected. Are there valid points, areas in which you need to improve? Or, could it be that the person who rejected you has doubts themselves? You have to prove yourself—to you, not anyone else. Perhaps the opportunity or relationship was not for you; keep knocking until the right door opens. Whatever the case maybe, make it your resolve never to give up. We hear this statement quite often, but what does it mean to never give up?

**Never Give Up:**

*To be persistent, to keep going, to believe in yourself, challenge yourself, keep learning, keep growing, work harder and smarter, being determined to keep trying until you reach your desired result*

Your attitude toward a goal will determine your end result. If you think you will never achieve a goal you probably will not, but if you have a mindset of never giving up you will most likely overcome any doubt that may come into your mind and succeed at achieving your goal. You may have to go back to the drawing board or take a different path all together, the key is to persist and keep going. When one door closes, dust your feet off and just go to the next one, do not take on a negative attitude allowing room for the seed of doubt to be planted—it is hard to uproot. How do you get pass doubt?

Get busy, take action, challenge yourself to prove doubt wrong. Focus on positioning yourself for success.

Prepare yourself for the next opportunity. Being prepared pushes doubt out, making room for opportunities to come your way. The truth is, you want to stay prepared, do not let up. When the door of opportunity opens, you can walk through with confidence rather than being caught off guard.

Being in an unfamiliar space and stepping out of your comfort zone can cause you to doubt yourself. It's ok to feel uncomfortable for a period of time until you adjust, that's why it's referred to as stepping outside your comfort zone. When you step into an unfamiliar space the seed of doubt wants to grow. It wants to push you back into your confined space. It wants to pull you back in the familiar place that you know. Doubt wants you to feel safe; it resists change.

You will feel uncomfortable when you make the decision to courageously, boldly, fearlessly step outside your comfort zone. The feeling of being uncomfortable will surface each time you go into another zone. As you continue to take steps, the uncomfortable phase will not last long; you realize it is a part of the growth process.

You will go through uncomfortable phases in life as you stretch yourself to new heights. Doubts will certainly surface, as you learn and grow, you will be able to let them go.

What are your lingering doubts when it comes to moving forward with your life?

_____

_____

_____

_____

# GARBAGEOUT

Why do the doubts exist?

_____

_____

_____

_____

_____

_____

How can you relinquish doubts?

_____

_____

_____

_____

_____

_____

Why are you determined to keep going despite any doubts that may try to surface?

_____

_____

_____

_____

_____

_____

_____

*You with little faith, why did you give way to doubt?*
~ Matthew 14:31

*You looked at the windstorm and became afraid.*

*As for your eyes straight ahead they should look, yes your own beaming eyes should gaze straight in front of you.*
~ Proverbs 4:25

# GARBAGEOUT

## OTHER PEOPLE'S PERCEPTIONS

Garbage can pile up because of negative people you allow to exist in your life. Not only do you have to let go of your own fears, doubts and insecurities, but you also must let go of the garbage other people try to project onto you. Many times we become afraid of what other people think, such as, that's a dumb idea, who do you think you are, you better stick to something safe. My advice to you is to go for what you want, do your research and get prepared for the next chapter in your life. People are entitled to their own thoughts and feelings you do not have to take them on as your truth. People will always have a perception about who you are and what you do—let them have it. What people say is not a strong enough reason for you to quit and conform to their wishes. They really aren't worth paying any attention; don't give them the time of day. Their words and opinions are not your reality.

If you notice you are making decisions based on what others think, ask yourself, "Why am I allowing this person to control my life?" In essence, that is what's happening. Now do you really think they care about how you are feeling? I will answer that for you, NO! So why are you allowing your thoughts, feelings, and behaviors to be manipulated by someone who has no regard for your feelings at all?

Move on and take back your control. Most people will not admit their true perception of you especially when it's negative. If you hear about negative comments that have been made, the majority will only admit that it was a misunderstanding and more than likely claim that you were the one that misunderstood, you were too sensitive or just took it the wrong way. You know the drill, do not allow what other people think or say interfere with what you have going on. Smile and keep on walking.

## *BE CLEAR AND CONFIDENT ABOUT*
## *WHO YOU ARE AND WHAT YOU WANT*

You do not need an apology or acknowledgement of any wrong. Most importantly, you do not need permission from anyone to live your life.

Now, instead of feeling angry when you think about or come into contact with this person, give yourself permission to feel free, alive and happy. If you are in a position where you can walk away from this person, do so, fast. If you happen to work with this person, limit your contact. Keep the conversation business only and if the conversation takes a turn for the negative, take a deep breath and look for an exit, you do not have to be rude; just say, "excuse me I have to take care of something," which you do—yourself.

## TOXIC PEOPLE DO NOT DESERVE YOUR TIME OR ENERGY

I call them energy zappers, gossipers, complainers, faultfinders; stay as far away from them as possible. Your life is not about pleasing everyone—that is impossible. Understand that you cannot please everyone and accept it. Do not let your life be about the hang-ups of other people.

Ask yourself the following questions:

Have I allowed other people's opinion to affect my decisions?

Yes or No.

If you answered yes to this question, think about a situation where you have let others affect your decisions—your life.

How did the situation work out for you?

_____

_____

_____

_____

_____

Going forward, how are you going to make decisions based on knowing who you are, what you want and where you want to go?

_____

_____

_____

_____

_____

Always keep your decisions in line with your core values. Seek advice from those you trust, but let the final decision be yours.

## EXCUSES, EXCUSES, EXCUSES

Excuses will never end as long as you keep making room for them to grow. There is no benefit to blaming your behavior or lack of success on anyone else, but yourself. Excuses will hang around as long as you let them. They will emerge at the most convenient time, exactly when you have something that needs to be done, that you do not really want to do. You are aware of the benefit of the job at hand, but the excuses keep coming, so you give in and do very little or nothing at all. You have heard the saying, "Excuses build bridges to nowhere." You are greater than your excuses.

### *EXPECT TO WIN, EXPECT TO DO GREAT THINGS*

When challenges arise expect to find a solution, know that obstacles can be knocked down, if you let go of the excuses. Instead of thinking of reasons why you cannot do something, think of reasons why you can do it. This is a part of the process of getting the garbage out. Avoid trying to accomplish your goals all at once. Break your goals up into pieces, instead of looking at it as a whole. Trying to do everything all at once can be overwhelming. That's why it is important to write a plan detailing exactly how you will get things done. Having a plan allows you to create a blueprint of the specific steps you need to take in order to bring you closer to accomplishing your goals. For instance, if you want to get the ball rolling to start your own business, you must write down a plan. Your plan does not have to be long and drawn out, keep it simple, do your research, start networking and explore your options. If you want to get out of debt, make an outline that details your spending habits and start making adjustments. It is not rocket science as to what needs to be done to reach your goals. You have to get rid of excuses and just do what it takes to get your desired outcome. This is called taking responsibility for your life. When you set a goal, it is important for your thoughts and actions to be in alignment. Make no room for excuses. Excuses throw you off course, pulling your thoughts in one direction and your actions in another; there is no agreement, which leads to no progress.

Get fed up. Sometimes to make changes in your life you have to get fed up with yourself. You have to take personal responsibility for your situation in order to make your life better. Excuses block your mind and stop you from achieving your goals and living your true life story.

### Be fed up with making excuses.
### What excuses do you need to stop making?

Be fed up with blaming others. When you waste time blaming others, you miss potential opportunities. Take responsibility—stop blaming the dissatisfaction with your life and your career on others, start taking yourself and your life seriously.

*BLAME GOES IN THE GARBAGE PILE*
*GARBAGE PARALYZES YOU, LET IT GO*

Ask yourself, what positive effects have I received from blaming others?

Has blaming others made your situation better or worse?

When you are too busy shifting blame, you expend time and energy in all the wrong places.

List the people you have been blaming for your current situation, what blame have you placed on them, and blame them no more.

_____

_____

_____

_____

_____

It is time for you to take control of your life. Take action to change course and transform your life.

What other excuses have you been holding onto? Write them down and let them go.

_____

_____

_____

_____

_____

Get fed up with yourself.

When are you going to take charge and make the necessary changes in your life to accomplish your goals? Don't get caught up in the blame game it is non-productive.

Focus on changing your response to life. Stop operating in victim mode and do something to change the course of your life—transform your challenges into to opportunities.

Take an honest look at the contribution you are making to what's going on in your life right now—are you where you want to be; if not do something about it!

Write down a goal you want to accomplish within the next 30 days.

_____

_____

_____

_____

_____

Find a quiet spot in the morning and evening and visualize the steps you need to take to make the vision you have for your life a reality. Do at least one thing a day to move you closer to accomplish your goals.

*IT IS TIME TO CLEAN HOUSE AND GET YOUR LIFE IN
ORDER; NO MORE EXCUSES*

## WHY WORRY

Worry causes one to grow anxious, to shut down, to be become afraid robbing one of strength and the initiative to take action. There is plenty to worry about, but the goal is not to let worry overtake you. Focus on the outcome you want, the solution. The solution grounds you and helps you put things into perspective, clearing your mind so that you can put an effective action plan in place. Worry usually makes the problem worse and blocks your mental space. Blocking the positive channels that could give you the solution needed to remedy the problem. You mentally become consumed with worry. Your thought process is focused on the worst case scenarios in this space, you are constantly thinking about the what ifs. Your mind is preoccupied with thoughts that cause more worry. This kind of thinking is unproductive.

What do you worry about the most? Do you worry about your relationships, money, work, etc.?

_____

_____

_____

_____

_____

What is your solution to worrying less?

_____

_____

_____

_____

_____

_____

How does worrying make you feel? Are you usually stressed out and anxious when you worry, do you constantly repeat your worries to others or do you shutdown.

_____

_____

_____

_____

_____

_____

When challenges arise in your life, instead of worrying, think about ways you can be proactive in finding a solution? List ways to focus on finding a solution.

_____

_____

_____

_____

_____

Has worrying helped you in the pass? Does worrying make you feel better or worse? Explain

_____

_____

_____

_____

_____

_____

What happens to your body when you worry? How does worrying affect your health?

_____

_____

_____

_____

_____

_____

_____

_____

_____

**Symptoms of Worry:**

Loss of concentration, irritability, restlessness, fatigue, heart palpitations, shortness of breath and anxiety; worry can even lead to a heart attack. You are putting your life at risk.

Worrying affects your overall ability to think clear; Worrying is like a weed that grows uncontrollable.

Pay attention to what triggers feelings of worry

How does worrying affect your mood? Do you get upset, afraid, anxious or depressed? Why?

_____

_____

_____

_____

_____

_____

Pay attention to your thoughts.

## Minimize worry:

- Identify the problem

- Brainstorm solutions

- Decide on a solution

- Identify the steps you are going to take

- Implement your solution

- Reflect on what really happens and what you can do better next time

You have to be in control when you are in a situation in which worrying starts to fester. Acknowledge the worry: say, "I am not going to use my time or energy on worrying, instead I will think of a solution." At this point, start thinking about options to handle the situation to gain control rather than worry. Begin putting an action plan in place then take action.

When the situation has been handled, consider what worried you so much, and then write down what really happened as your model to handle future situations successfully.

Repeat this process when a situation arises that may cause you to worry until you begin to worry less. Worrying empowers the things that you fear. The goal is to decrease worrying and keep the GarbageOut!

*"There isn't enough room in your mind for worry and faith, you have to decide which one will live there"*
~ Unknown

Have faith that you have the strength to move mountains, "If your faith were the size of a mustard seed you could say to this mountain, 'Move from here to there,' and it would move, nothing would be impossible for you." ~Matthew 17:20

### Imagine not climbing but moving the mountain

You have the power to move mountain like obstacles that try to block your path. Do not give your power away to worry. Take a deep breath and take charge of your life. Yes, it is going to be challenging, but you can do it. When you believe anything is possible and you let go of worry and focus on the solution; you can move mountains.

## MENTAL HOUSECLEANING

Our physical health is directly related to our mental and emotional health—they go hand in hand.

If you find yourself constantly replaying bad experiences, reliving the past, making the same mistakes over and over again, resisting change; it's time to put a routine in place to remove the garbage blocking your path.

### Here are a few suggestions:

- Ask Yourself Honest Questions and Give Honest Answers

- Build Self Worth

- Mental Exercise

- Physical Exercise

- Reflect on Life Lessons

- Develop Strong Reasoning Skills

- Keep a Journal

We will elaborate on each point later in the book.

When you are mentally living in a garbage dump, sometimes it can seem impossible to dig your way out. Start throwing away one piece at a time; replace your fears, doubts and insecurities with something new and uplifting. When garbage starts to creep in challenge yourself to redirect your thoughts.

Then gradually move up to throwing away bags of garbage, standup for yourself, stand in your power and say, "I am not taking this garbage anymore, it's time to stop looking back and move forward; it's time to clean house." When your garbage can becomes full at home, you know it is time to take out the garbage.

When you feel your heart getting heavy, you feel weighed down you know it is time to throw away your mental and emotional garbage. You know you have let the garbage stay to long when it starts to stink: depression can start to sink in; holding onto mental garbage can cause you to become easily agitated, sick, drained, sluggish, stuck, unable to function or think clearly.

*Throw your garbage out daily, purge negative thoughts; create space to grow, to feel alive*

## CAN YOU FEEL THE DIFFERENCE A CLEAN HOUSE MAKES?

*A clean house requires routine cleaning*

Just as you would physically clean your house, you should physically clean your mind. Thoughts of fear, doubt and insecurity can consume you keeping you confined, constrained and confused.

Let your experiences be exactly what they are—experiences. You will have good experiences and bad experiences. Do not allow bad experiences to stagnate you, learn from them and move forward. Allow your good experiences to propel you to new heights. Know that your life is what you make of it. Work through difficult times and know that they will not last forever.

## How Garbage Shows Up In Your Life

Stress
Guilt
Uncontrollable Anger
Weight Gain
Depression
Financial Issues
Health Problems
Procrastination
Blame
Fear
Excuses
Regret
Doubt
Insecurity
Worry
Feeling of Being Stuck

## What Garbage Do You Need to Dump and Leave!

Write down the garbage you need to throw away and simple let
go

# GARBAGEOUT

## THE TURMOIL WITHIN

Being consumed with thoughts that create fear, doubt and insecurity tear you down and limit your success causing you to be in a constant state of turmoil. There is a war going on within you, each side refusing to surrender. The fight is real!

The glimmer of hope that is dimly lit is fighting for survival wanting you to wake up, take control, see the good and take notice of the lesson. The glimmer of hope wants you to find your gift, talents and most importantly—you. The very being of who you are is hidden within, buried underneath the garbage that keeps seeping in, telling you to be afraid, that you are not worthy, that you are not good enough; leading you to feelings of worthlessness, inadequacy, lack of confidence all of which fuel destructive thoughts and behavior; burying you deeper and deeper under the cloud of despair. Why do you allow these thoughts to keep seeping in, controlling every step that you take?

*The garbage that has accumulated*
*is keeping you in shackles*
*daring you to fight for your freedom*

The fight wages on with each side fighting to take over your domain: the glimmer of hope and freedom verses the despair and fear. Each side is fighting to take over your mind, your heart, your soul, the very being of who you are.

The voices of fear, insecurity and doubt keep getting louder with a mission to take over your life. Why do you hold these voices so dearly, paying attention to there every word? The aim is to minimize your very existence. Can't you see that they are suffocating you, taking the breath of life from you, distracting you from being who you really are, convincing you to give up on you?

Now is the time for you to dig deep and muster up the strength to fight for your dignity, self-respect—your life. Stand up and shout back even louder, I am in control; fear will not hold me back. Look fear in the eye and say, "MOVE, I am worthy, mistakes have taught me lessons, and failure has provided the steppingstones to my success. The confidence I have found has made me far from inadequate. I am more than enough!" Shout, "I am free to be me. I am free!"

Do feelings of fear, insecurity and doubt over past mistakes surface over and over again in your life? Explain.

_____

_____

_____

_____

_____

_____

_____

_____

What specific fears, insecurities and doubts continue to linger in your mind?

_____

_____

_____

_____

_____

_____

How has holding onto fear, insecurity and doubt (garbage) affected your life?

_____

_____

_____

_____

_____

_____

What would be the benefits of letting go?

_____

_____

_____

_____

_____

What would you be doing right now if you didn't allow fear, doubt and insecurity to control your life?

_____

_____

_____

_____

_____

_____

## **GET THE GARBAGEOUT AND CREATE SPACE FOR:**

Joy
Peace
Love
Acceptance
Self-Control
Faith
Forgiveness
Good Health
A Clear Vision of your Future
Self-Respect
Feeling of Accomplishment
Patience
Kindness
Freedom
Compassion
Strength
Growth
Success

And so much more

What do you want to create space for in your life?

## DANGER Of HOLDING ON

The danger of holding onto fear, insecurity and doubt prevent you from being fully present in your life, discovering your passion, talents, gift, accomplishing your goals, and growing into all you are capable of being.

When you hold onto thoughts and feelings that weigh you down, you cloud your vision, creating a false perception of how you view yourself, which materializes as false evidence appearing real. The false perception of self leads to feelings of inadequacy, even though you are far from being inadequate. You begin to lack the motivation to be more; stagnation sets in producing stress, anxietyty even hopelessness.

*If you struggle to let go, imagine how you would feel in a year, five years when you look back, you haven't grown, you are still standing in the same place*

Allowing mental garbage to accumulate creates confusion and turmoil all around you, inside and out. You have no idea where you are, where you are going or what you want out of life, there is a mental block that needs to be cleared.

Letting go of self-defeating thoughts frees up space to create clarity and structure. Clarity brings about freedom. Freedom to be yourself and freedom to go after what you want.

### LETTING GO IS A DIFFICULT TASK

In fact, its probably one of the hardest things you will ever have to do. Letting go of mental garbage involves retraining your mind to think in a different way. Your fears, doubts and insecurities can hold you captive. Restraining you from finding out what is waiting for you on the other side. You have to dig deep and find the courage to let go.

Instead of focusing on the obstacles, focus on your intention. What do you want to accomplish? When you peel away all the layers and get to the real issues of what is holding you back; you begin to understand the danger of holding onto fear, doubt and insecurity. These are the very things that are blocking your path, creating the illusion that you are not capable of starting your own business, writing a book, making a career change, becoming debt free or losing weight.

Fear will rule your very exist if you allow it. Doubt will override your true judgment if you give it a voice and insecurity will push you in a corner. So, what do you want? You have to find balance in your life. You have to make the decision as to what you hold onto and let go. If you try to hold onto everything you are going to be off balance same is true if you let go of everything, there has to be an equalizing—balance. Things you hold onto have to serve a purpose otherwise, let go. You have to train your mind to think in a different way to let go of thoughts that are sabotaging you life.

## MEDIATE ON THE FOLLOWING SENRIOS?

What do I truly want out of life?

Do you want more freedom?

Maybe you want to turn your existing passion into a new career. Perhaps what you really want is a loving relationship.

*ACKNOWLEDGE WHAT YOU WANT*
*ACCEPT IT AND VALIDATE IT*

Honor who you are by not holding onto thoughts that devalue your worth—your life. Next, tap into your creative energy. Imagine that whatever you want is available to you, in an infinite number of ways. Visualize how many different ways you can have what you really want. I encourage you to write down your vision in as much detail as possible. Bring your vision to life.

When you use your imagination in this way, you open yourself up to numerous possibilities. Mediation is a powerful tool to transform your thinking, attitude and perception, enabling you to let go and move forward. Why place yourself in an imaginary box when there are so many opportunities waiting for you to respond?

The danger of holding on is that you miss out on life. Holding on places limits. Letting go releases you from limitations, clearing a path for you to explore your dreams, desires, discover your passion, but most importantly you gain the freedom to discover you!

What feelings are keeping you hidden?

_____

_____

_____

_____

_____

_____

_____

Are you living up to your worth? Explain why or why not

_____

_____

_____

_____

_____

_____

_____

_____

What makes you truly happy?

_____

_____

_____

_____

What are the dangers of holding on? Why is it important to break free? Explain in detail

_____

_____

_____

_____

_____

_____

_____

_____

_____

_____

_____

_____

## SICK AND TIRED

Have you ever just been sick and tired of being sick and tired? Personally, I just got sick and tired of the garbage telling me what I could not do, putting fears, doubts and insecurities in front. Remember, fear is meant to be conquered, doubt can be diminished, and insecure feelings can be overcome.

Who cares about what people will say? You cannot please everyone and neither should you try.

Now, what is next? Put on a new attitude, know your worth, live your truth, and truly believe you can do whatever you set your mind to. Call the shot and go for it.

Sometimes you have to get sick and tired of being sick and tired in order to do something to transform your life.

If you are sick and tired, prove it!

# CHAPTER TWO

# FINDING YOUR WAY

## LIFE SPEAKS

Are you listening? Creation speaks of life. The rustling of the leaves speak of movement, not standing still. The statue of the trees speaks of strength, fortitude and courage. The sky speaks of unlimited potential. The stars speak of the twinkle in your eye when you have found the purpose that makes your life worth living. The moon speaks of completeness. The rays of the sun speak of caring. Life's creations confidently speak to you sharing its sheer worth, exquisite beauty, guiding wisdom and enduring faith. What are you saying in return?

Are you speaking of courage, faith and strength? Are you listening to life's wisdom trying to guide you to step out on faith, rather than to stand still? It's saying you are worthy and longing to reveal the beauty you have on the inside so that you can express it on the outside. Wanting you to be a complete being.

Have you succumbed to the darkness minimizing your worth, living in fear, doubting your talents, draining your strength and overshadowing your gift? Are you listening as life speaks, trying to help you find your way?

What do you need to clear from your life to hear what life is truly trying to tell you?

What is your life trying to say to you?

*Life is trying to tell you how wonderful you are—listen.*

## CHANGE YOUR RESPONSE TO LIFE

Change your response to life; use each experience to learn something new, to take away the lesson and to grow. Your response to life experiences shape how you see yourself, how you feel about who you are, whether you are moving forward or standing still in your life. How you respond will determine your level of awareness, which in turn determines your level of growth.

Your past does not define you. Everyday, you have an opportunity to create your defining moment and truly start living life. Move forward with a positive view of yourself. Tell yourself, "I do deserve this and even if I do fail, the world will not end; I will just start again and again and again until I get it right."

*The greatest failure in life is to quit; starting over one more time will only lead you closer to success*

Be aware of your surroundings; be aware of the emotions that certain situations will evoke. Pay attention to the things in your life that generate positive emotions. Pay attention to things in your life that generate negative emotions. Life presents a variety of experiences to help shape and mold you into the person you are supposed to be. There will be setbacks, opportunities, successes, disappointments, victories and failures; you have to choose to grow from life's experiences whether good or bad. Choose to respond from a place of awareness; from the pain you can learn what not to do, to appreciate life—not to take it for granted; when you experience joy you have the opportunity to extend gratitude and to continue doing things that will create more joy.

The event or situation should not dictate your response to life; the outcome you want should be your focus—think from the end. When you become upset over a situation, do you want to become enraged, out of control or do you want to remain calm and make decisions that will make you better. Be determined to settle matters quickly, you do not want to remain in a provoked state. Seek peace and purse it, it's something you have to work at.

To let go of anger focus your thoughts on cultivating qualities that will make you a better person. Qualities that will help you respond from a place of control instead of from a place that is spiraling out of control. Your response to life determines your level of happiness and success in all areas of your life. Let go of the garbage, it's not worth it. When you change your response to life, your life will change.

How do you response to setbacks and disappointments that occur in your life? Why?

_____

_____

_____

_____

_____

_____

_____

## GARBAGE OUT

Does your response to setbacks and disappointments leave you feeling energized or drained? If your response leaves you drain, how would changing your response to life benefit you?

_____

_____

_____

_____

_____

_____

_____

_____

_____

_____

_____

_____

## HAVE COURAGE

Courage is to act despite fear, uncertainty or even opposition. Have the courage to act with boldness, to be strong, to be brave, to dare to live your story! Once you take the first step, then the second step, by the third step your power will start to kick in—you are building your momentum to courageously take intentional action to live your truth.

Making the decision to grow despite challenges requires bold action. Life will present many opportunities for you to act with courage and face your fears head on. At different stages in your life you will encounter challenges that will encourages you to grow. It is up to you to accept the challenge or not, having the courage to grow is not easy. Fight feelings of helplessness, gain control over your thoughts and break the cycle, stop allowing fear to rule your life. Choose courage—take steps that will make you stronger and braver. Make a conscious decision to courageously step up and take responsibility for your life! Your thoughts can make you believe you are not capable of success. Pay attention to the thoughts that you nurture.

*Where are your thoughts leading you?*

*Are they empowering you to act with courage or shrink back in fear?*

It takes courage to believe in you, to trust in yourself, to achieve what appears in the moment to be impossible. People will try to put you in a box and leave you there. It takes courage to break free and be different. Yes people will talk about you, some who were once close to you will desert you, but that's ok.

Be prepared to be a solo act for a while, if you have support that's great. Just never give up on you!

Break free and be determined not to be boxed in by the perceptions of others. The path you have chosen is not an easy road to travel. There will be many bumps along the way. Sometimes you may want to turn back. When you allow fear to control you—you are giving away your power. Have the courage to persevere. Start visualizing your success. See yourself taking intentional steps to reach your goals. Act on the belief that anything is possible because it is, believe this with all your heart. Move toward your goals. Know that you will find a way.

## HAVE THE COURAGE TO TAKE ON LIFE

Be determined to grow. Growth gives you new life, a new beginning, a fresh start and a breath of clean air. Growth filters your life of doubt, insecurity and fear; building your confidence with each step you take. Empowering you to act with courage, creating space for your truth to shine through.

Before gold becomes pure, it has to be filtered of its impurities. The refining reveals the pure gold and removes the dross (impurities). As you grow, you are being transformed; your courageous steps refine you. Your willpower to respond to life with courage is being strengthen, you are being refined; step up and have the courage to shine.

Having the courage to grow starts the refinement process; with one step from you, the filtering begins. Have courage, keep growing until you become refined and transformed into pure gold.

*Be Courageous and Strong* ~ Joshua 10:25

## CONNECTING THE DOTS

Your vision of your life starts with an idea that creates a mental picture of your future. Your vision begins to mentally take shape when you take intentional steps to connect the dots.

A picture is nice to look at, but you have to create a plan to connect the dots and bring your vision to life. Your vision can easily become blurred with all the mental garbage you have collected over the years. If you do nothing with your vision, it remains a figment of your imagination. It gets lost. You first create your vision with your mind, and then you have to live it. Your vision has to be so real to the point you are driven to breathe life into your vision—you can see it, taste it, feel it and touch it. This is when you know you have taken life lessons and applied them in your life. You develop a clear picture of where you want to go in life and you begin taking action to bring your story to life. As you connect the dots you are discovering who you really are.

**CONNECT THE DOTS:**

GET THE GARBAGEOUT fear, doubt, insecurity—Clear your path

ORGANIZE YOUR THOUGHTS write them down, organizing your thoughts on paper will help you to organize them in your mind

DEVELOP A PLAN put a specific plan in place to help you connect the dots, if you want to make a career change or write a book. What specific steps do you have to take? Map out a plan, Set priorities and deadlines

PUT YOUR PLAN IN MOTION act on your vision, write down action steps you will complete each day and start each day with the determination to complete each step

BE PRESENT pay attention to your surroundings, those whom you associate with, take note of your failures and successes, learn from good experiences and bad experiences

MAKE WISE DECISIONS make decisions that reflect your truth and make you feel great, stay true to yourself. Do not compromise your standards

When you start to pay attention, you realize that all of the things you have experienced in your life have gotten you to the point where you are now. You are connecting the dots.

Applying the things you have learned in life opens up the path for you to grow. As positive change begins to take place, your life takes a turn for the better, pointing you in a direction to live your life purpose.

The goal is to have a clear mental vision of what you want out of life, then to go after it. This starts with having a crystal clear picture of who you are. Knowing who you are gives rise to clearly knowing what you want.

A vision is just a vision until you connect the dots and make it a reality.

What vision do you have for your life? Write your vision in one sentence

_____

_____

_____

_____

What's your plan to make your vision a reality? You need a plan to get from where you are now to where you want to go.

_____

_____

_____

_____

_____

_____

_____

_____

_____

_____

_____

_____

_____

## LIFE'S JOURNEY

*Now I would like to tell you a little bit about my journey—about my story*

One thing I have learned is that life has many twist and turns; there are so many directions to choose from. Upon graduating from high school we all are faced with a major decision that most teenager are not equip to make—what are you going to do with the rest of your life. I decided to major in Business—I have always envisioned myself as a business owner, but first I wanted to climb the corporate ladder, so I thought.

While attending college I worked as a bank teller. I have had the opportunity to cross train and learn about many different areas in banking. Once I completed college I started working for a technology company, as a project coordinator within six months I was promoted to a sales account manager.

An opportunity became available and I begin working for a major corporation, as a revenue analysis, there were quite a few egos to deal with on this job, and a lot of backbiting and this is were my desire to climb the corporate ladder diminished, I was laid off from this position, looking back it was if life was telling me—you have learned enough from corporate America, it is time for you to move on. Around this time I started contemplating transitioning into education and becoming a teacher in addition to my degree in Business I also have a minor in education—I never considered teaching as a career. At the suggestion of a friend I obtained a minor in education, he said, "It would be good to have options." Looking at it from that perspective it seemed to be a wise choice. To my surprise I thoroughly enjoyed taking the education courses, during my last quarter we were assigned to shadow a teacher in the local school system. I had to create and teach my own lesson plans, I was assigned to tutor three students who needed extra help in their course work. During the time I was there, their grades improved tremendously. The students began to focus more in school and completing their homework. I have to say teaching is definitely a career that can make you feel like you are making a difference in someone's life.

Now as I continued to contemplate whether or not I would transition into teaching; I begin to ask myself a few questions. Do you really want to be in a classroom all day? What did you enjoy about teaching? My conclusion was—No, I really don't think I want to be in a classroom all day and what I truly enjoyed about teaching was tutoring and the personal satisfaction I received from seeing individual students' progress and their confidence growing as they began to trust themselves. The students lacked the recognition and the feeling that they were enough, but once they received the needed attention, the reassurance—they begin to flourish.

What I learned from this experience is that we all need recognition, reassurance and to feel valued. As we grow into adulthood the reality is the recognition, reassurance and the value has to come from ourselves the majority of the time. That's why it is important to build your inner strength. Recognize your true worth, reassure yourself that you are enough and value the person that you are. Never minimize your existence.

Being a teacher can be very rewarding, I had to remind myself that my goal has always been to start my own business, my wheels began to turn. In corporate America I had acquired skills in marketing, sales, networking, accounting, project management, just to name a few. Now how could I combine the skills I had acquired with my desire to start my own business and my interest in education. When I begin to pay attention to the things I enjoyed and the things that brought me personal satisfaction things begin to unfold. I made the decision that if I was going to climb any ladder it was going to be my own. Over the course of 10 years I have had many business ideas that did not pan out, but I never gave up the dream of owning my own business.

One day I was doing some spring cleaning. As I was cleaning and going through boxes, I had been meaning to go through for the longest, I came across a note written by my 11th grade literature teacher, Ms. Taylor, she had attached a note to one of my papers, it stated, "You are going to be a great writer someday." I couldn't believe it. I beamed with happiest on the inside. Ms. Taylor thought that much of me. I could even remember telling some of my peers about the note. They didn't believe me, so I showed them, with pride!

Just think I dredged having to take her class. She was labeled as mean and hard. She had a very serious demeanor and her voice said, "I don't play." I actually ended up seating in the front seat. I thought I was going to die, as you see I didn't, I am still here. I ended up really enjoying her class, even though she did scare me a little. I didn't keep the paper, I wish I had, but I kept the note. When I look at it even today it makes me smile and say she thought that much of me. As I continued going through boxes I came across some poems, letters I had written, even a few lines of a book I had attempted to write, I said, "These are pretty good." I had forgotten all about by goal of writing a book.

*Distractions have a way of clouding our vision, piling up and hiding our talents and gift; we just have to clear our mental path, to find them*

As I continued reading some of the stories, the desire to write again was rekindled. The weird thing is I never cared for writing very much; Ms. Taylor lit a spark in me that never went out, dimmed at times by the distractions of life, but still grasping for air waiting for me to take notice. I knew something was there that was longing to come out.

The more I would meditate and write, the more the ideas started to emerge; I began to take notice of a creative side, ideas flowing, coming together to make a complete picture excited me, giving me the longing to create more.

One night I began writing. There were many topics that came to mind, none of them felt quite right. I decided to call it a night and attempted to go to sleep; disturbing negative thoughts begin to flow through my mind.

What are you thinking, you can't write a book?
Who's going to read it?
Nobody is going to take you serious?
Who do you think you are?

What disturbing negative thoughts do you need to let go?

_____

_____

_____

_____

_____

_____

_____

# GARBAGEOUT

## THERE IS GOING TO BE A STRUGGLE WHEN
## YOU ARE SHIFTING, THERE WILL BE RESISTANCE

As I laid in bed the mental resistance continued then an internal scream came out—one like I had never felt before, "GARBAGEOUT!" Instantly I sat up on the bed I felt a load lifted. Then a light bulb went off I said, "That's it, "GarbageOut" *is* the title!"

"GarbageOut" was born

I knew all those negative thoughts held no real value, but for a moment I was questioning myself. You have to realize that your thoughts are very powerful and the affect that mental garbage has on you. Be determined to live your true story. Take a moment, sit still and listen and you will find your way.

As my life continues to unfold it becomes clearer as to what direction I should be going in—a direction that will allow me to continuously grow and make a difference in the lives of others.


## THOUGHTS ARE VERY POWERFUL
## FIGHT FOR CONTROL

~P. Ashworth

## BE BOLD

To be bold is to live in color. Not to hide or shrink back. To be confident about the choices you make and the steps you take. Not looking for permission from others to be you—to use your gift. Be proud of your uniqueness, your talents and your skills. Boldly live your truth out loud. Let your light shine and find your way.

Taking the leap to live your true story requires boldness. You are going to face challenges that will test your endurance. Those closest to you at the moment maybe the very ones that challenge you the most, projecting their negative thoughts, planting seeds of doubt, causing you to second guess yourself; pulling you backwards instead of propelling you forward. You have to make a bold decision. Do you limit your association with these individuals or do you need to remove them from your life altogether?

Let me share a story with you, it's actually a fable—a story that teaches life lessons. Most of you have probably heard this one before, but I don't think it can be told enough because you truly need to understand the impact your association has on your life.

A farmer found an egg. He put it with his chickens and soon the egg hatched. This bird looked a little different from the others. It was an eagle. The young eagle grew up with all the other chickens and whatever they did, the eagle, did too. He really thought he was a chicken.

Then one day an eagle flew over the barnyard. The eagle looked up and wondered, "What kind of animal is that? How graceful, powerful and free." Then he asked another chicken, "What is that?" The chicken replied, "Oh, that is an eagle, you don't have to worry yourself about that; you will never be able to fly. The eagle belongs in the sky. We belong on the ground, we are just chickens." The eagle went back to scratching the ground. He continued to behave like a chicken for the rest of his chicken life. He died, never knowing the life he could have lived.

**But, what if the eagle had someone in his corner that believed in him? What if the eagle believed in himself? Here's another version of the fable. Which one would you rather live?**

A naturalist came to the chicken farm to see if what he had heard about an eagle acting like a chicken was really true. He knew that an eagle was powerful and great. He was surprised to see the eagle strutting around the chicken coop, pecking at the ground, acting like a chicken. The farmer explained to the naturalist that this bird was no longer an eagle; he was a chicken. The eagle had been around chickens for so long he now believed he was a chicken.

The naturalist knew there was more to this great bird than his actions showed in this moment. He was born an eagle and had the heart of an eagle and nothing could change that. The man lifted the eagle onto the fence surrounding the chicken coop and said, "You are an eagle, stretch out your wings and fly." The eagle moved slightly, only to look at the man then glance down at his home among the chickens in the chicken coop where he was comfortable. He jumped off the fence and continued doing what chickens do. The farmer said, "I told you he was a chicken."

The naturalist returned the next day and tried again to convince the farmer and the eagle that the eagle was born for something greater. He took the eagle to the top of the farmhouse and said to him, "You are an eagle, stretch out your wings and fly." The eagle looked at the man, jumped from the man's arm onto the roof of the farmhouse and back to the chicken coop he went.

Knowing how powerful and magnificent eagles are, the naturalist asked the farmer to let him try one more time. He would return the next day and prove that this bird was an eagle. The farmer, convinced otherwise, said, "It is a chicken."

The naturalist returned the next morning to the chicken farm and took the eagle and the farmer some distance away from the chicken coop to the edge of a high mountain. They could not see the farm or the chicken coop from this new setting. The man held the eagle on his arm and pointed high into the sky. He said, "You are an eagle, stretch out your wings and fly." This time the eagle stared skyward into the bright sun, without looking back. The eagle straighten his powerful body; stretched out his massive wings, moving slowly at first, then boldly picking up his momentum; like the mightiness of an eagle he began to soar; taking ownership of the open sky—of his life.

**Sometimes you will have to go for it alone, that's ok, if you have faith you are never alone**

Are you going to live your life as a chicken or an eagle, the choice is up to you. Eagles boldly soar, chickens hangout in chicken coops all day. Inside you know if you are an eagle. When you boldly accept the call to be you, your path opens up. Clearing a way for you to make the next bold move.

*Dare yourself to take the leap, if you fall*
*be bold and get back up and try again and again*
*and again until you get the flow of life and soar*

**Life calls for bold action.**

**Are you up for the challenge?**

**Will you take the leap to boldly live your truth?**

## ACCEPTANCE

When you accept your gift and your talents you are completely accepting yourself—you feel complete. When you become truly aware of who you are. You know where you are in space and time. In the truest sense you have awaken. There will be no challenge you can't handle; you will find a way. When you take the initiative to live your life with courage, boldness and fearlessnes; no limits will be placed on you—fear, doubt, insecurity will no longer control you. You accept your gift, talents and you are thankful and willingly to share what has been freely given to you.

If you are in a place where you feel unworthy, afraid or scared of others people's reaction? It's time to let go and accept you!

### *TRAIN YOUR MIND TO WORK FOR YOU*

You have the power to let go of unwanted, harmful thoughts that take away your self-worth and keep you trapped in the past, unable to move. Thoughts that encourage you to overeat and not workout—replaying the same excuses: I am too tired, too busy; I will never lose this weight. Thoughts that constantly say I will never get out of debt or this is over my head. You have the power to get out of financial debt—know it, feel it, believe it, and start creating your financial plan. You have to think it, truly believe it, and take steps to achieve it. Don't just let your life be about mistakes, learn from them. Focus on the bigger picture. Strive to become a better decision-maker.

You can train your mind to do anything: to be strong or weak, to live with fear or courage, to be a victim or fearlessly claim your victory, to allow doubt to suppress you or boldness to propel you forward, to give into challenges or fight to overcome them. How you respond or react to life depends primarily on your mental strength to successfully handle life's challenges. When you fall will you get back up? We all need encouragement sometimes to pick us up, to give us the strength to keep going.

You must give yourself space to think, plan, and grow without unnecessary distractions. Be the driving force behind your thoughts; be in control of your domain, let go of the garbage.

What thoughts are distracting you from truly living your life?

_____

_____

_____

_____

_____

_____

_____

_____

_____

# GARBAGEOUT

What steps are you going to take to get rid of thoughts that block you from accepting who you are?

_____

_____

_____

_____

_____

_____

_____

_____

_____

_____

_____

_____

## ONE OF THE MOST IMPORTANT
## RELATIONSHIPS YOU CAN HAVE

One of the most important relationships you can have is the one you have with yourself. When you are constantly judging, comparing, critiquing and devaluing yourself; the question is raised, do you really like yourself? You tell yourself that you would never think such a thing, but then you are constantly telling yourself, I'm not good enough, I'm too fat, I'm not smart enough, I could never do that. In reality your thoughts are telling you that you do not value yourself that much causing you to settle for something less than your best.

Self-defeating thoughts can be interwoven into your everyday thinking to the point where you do not even realize the damage you are doing to yourself mentally and physically. Most people do not realize that self-defeating thoughts are one of the main reasons you continue to fall short of reaching your goals, whether it is to lose weight, become debt free, start a business or organize your home. It is never going to happen for you because mental garbage is clouding your vision and blocking your path. Unconsciously, mental garbage builds up day after day month after month and year after year. Flooding your mind with thoughts that beat you down and hide your true worth.

Your mind has to be strengthen in the same way your body is strengthen through exercise. To get the most benefit from a mental workout, you must eliminate the mental garbage that places limits on you. To be the best you can be, you have to be mentally fit. How you take care of yourself shows how much you value the relationship you have with yourself. The way you think has everything to do with where you are right now in your life.

When you are conscious of the damage negative thoughts cause in your life, you can start the process of freeing yourself by getting rid of them. Be in control of your thoughts; do not allow your thoughts to control you. Yes, you have the power to control your thoughts, use it.

*Let go of thoughts that place limits on your life*

*Do not make room for thoughts that de-value you*

*Listen to your instincts: do not allow self-defeating thoughts to force you into an undesired direction or into something that just does not feel right*

**You will stumble many times. You may even fall back into the old way of thinking momentarily. The key is to readjust and get back on track as fast as possible.**

When you truly listen to what is going on in your life, you will know when you are going in the right or wrong direction. There will be an absence of constant judgmental noise because you have deceased the volume of the noise, although it is still there, it is not dominating the conversation; it is gradually being quieted and removed.

Allow yourself to be invigorated by life's challenges not beat down, because life can sure give you a beating. You will continue to come out all bruised and battered if you continue to put yourself in the same situation over and over again. Until you finally realize it is time to do something different, you will continue to get the same results. Different results will require a different way of thinking and a different way of doing things.

When your mental power—your thinking ability, is strengthen, you fortify yourself to press on and not give up. When you make the decision to make a mental adjustment and readjust as needed, you will begin to make a shift in your life that will give you the courage to standup to life's challenges; the courage to accept change. You need to be bold in order to truly accept who you are.

Obstacles that you encounter in life can affect your thinking for better or worse. Are you strong enough mentally to stay focused despite mental distractions or will you allow mental garbage to take control? No, I can't do it, it is just too hard, I am not strong enough! You can either decide to accept these mental distractions that can lead to defeat or you can choose to think, I can handle anything that comes my way. This may seem very simple, but your thoughts mentally train your mind. It takes hard work to get to this point mentally and actually follow through; you have to remember that you have been thinking a certain way for a long time. Time and effort has to be put into training your mind to get rid of damaging mental dialogue that causes mental garbage to pile up.

*You can recreate your life by changing the way you think, and the only way to change the way you think is to let go of the garbage that is keeping your mind captive.*

## Start the process of letting go

Focus on Your Strengths

Embrace Your Power

Do Not Let Your Past Limit Your Future

Life Is Change—Accept It

Getting the garbage out helps you create harmony between your mental, physical, spiritual, and emotional being; a merger has to take place. You have the ability to create whatever you want in your life. Your success is based on the choices you make and the action you take. Be on a mission to connect with the most important person in your life, you.

What are 5 things you like about yourself? Now build upon them.

_____

_____

_____

_____

_____

_____

_____

# FIND YOUR PLACE

A place where you can be at peace
Let your hair down; put your feet up and relax
Move to and fro; with ease despite challenges
Embrace your accomplishments
Learn from mistakes and keep on living
A place where you can learn and grow
Have you found your place

A place where you can be confident in your own right
Sit still and clear your mind
Laugh out loud
Cry and not feel shame
Feel secure
A place where you can create a new beginning
Have you found your place

A place called LIFE
A place where you can openly express your true feelings
Ask for a helping hand
Live and thrive
Conquer your fears
A place where you can truly live your life without regret
Let Go and Find Your Place

What place are you trying to discover
A place to live and thrive
A place to conquer your fears
A place to create a new beginning
A place to sit still and clear your mind

~P. Ashworth

Share your story at www.garbageoutdaily.com

**THE ONLY WAY TO TRULY DISCOVER
MEANING AND PURPOSE IN LIFE IS TO
CLAIM YOUR FREEDOM**

~P. Ashworth

# CHAPTER THREE

# BE DISCIPLINED, BE FOCUSED

## SET YOUR STORY IN MOTION

If you want to be a writer, write; if you want to lose weight, start exercising and making better food choices; if you want to get out of debt, make a budget, stick to it, and put a little extra toward credit cards and bills; if you want to start a business, write your ideas down, do your research, and write a business plan; if you want to make a career change, prepare yourself, get the training you need to make the transition, sell your strengths, and be willing to learn the rest. If you don't succeed the first time, try a different path, until you find one that works for you. Have the courage to keep going. Boldly putting one foot in front of the other is the key to bringing about your success. Keep your story in motion; be disciplined, be focused.

Be determined to keep going. In life you will experience disappointment, you will fail from time to time. It doesn't mean you are a failure, it just means things didn't work out with a particular plan or idea. Just try something new, improve your idea, make a new plan, remember to learn from your previous mistakes and keep it moving.

*Lesson.* A failed plan is a failed plan. Accept that things didn't work out this go round, just pick up the lesson and fearlessly forge ahead.

### *IT IS ALL ABOUT YOUR COMMITMENT LEVEL*

Let's face it, if you are not truly committed, change is short-term. Real change requires commitment.

If you want real change then you have to be committed to developing your strengths, overcoming your weaknesses and taking ownership of your life.

What does change mean to you? Do you see change as having a positive or negative influence on your life?

_____

_____

_____

_____

_____

_____

_____

_____

To change—to grow—to become better

The only person you can change is you

Change can open your eyes to new opportunities

Change can be the best thing that ever happen to you

Real change takes effort—the amount of effort you put forth will determine your outcome. Your life is in your hands.

What does commitment mean to you?

_____

_____

_____

_____

_____

_____

Commitment can be liken to a promise that you make to yourself

**Repeat the following three statements:**

I promise myself to do everything in my power to accomplish my goals

I promise myself to stay focused and not allow unexpected challenges to knock me off track

I promise myself that I will take responsibility for my life and live my truth

Keep your promises to yourself

Real commitment requires heartfelt desire and dedication.

You will deal with garbage both physically and mentally every single day of your life. How you handle all the garbage that arises as you try to accomplish your goals is the deciding factor as to whether or not you will succeed.

Once your desire has set in and you are determined to accomplish your goals, you must be willing to dedicate time, energy and resources to see it through. Desire starts mentally as the thoughts start flowing; your aspirations begin to take root. Your desire drives your commitment level. How bad do you want to achieve your goal?

Now is the time to get rid of your old way of thinking, thinking that has only produced short-term results. Your desire has to be so strong that it quiets negative thoughts that create doubt, fear and insecurity. Tell yourself, "This is something I really want to accomplish." If this is one of your passions, the desire will be so strong that you will think about it when you wake up and go to sleep.

Letting go of fear, doubt and insecurity ensures that your desire to make changes to accomplish your goal is firmly planted. It is up to you to decide whether or not you will reach your goal. Having the desire to do something is only the first step to real change and living the life you want to live.

Now that the desire has taken root, you have to act, you have to be dedicated for long–term change to occur. Being 100 percent dedicated to the process gives you the backbone to stand on your own two feet. Be dedicated to making a plan and sticking to it. Make adjustments wherever necessary. Dedication doesn't happen overnight. It is a journey and with each step you will increase your level of commitment to the process. Dedication encompasses fortitude, staying power and the will to persevere.

Be dedicated to thinking things through:

- Plan

- Research

- Execute

Be determined not to quit. Dedication reinforces your level of commitment to succeed, giving you the strength to get up over and over again. Know that you are creating a better you with each try. Remember that change is about growth. Do not stop too soon when change is in progress; push past the awkward stage of unfamiliarity. Change will take you through stages that will make you feel uncomfortable. Do not give into fear. Fear plants the seed of doubt, which causes feelings of insecurity. Be determined not to shrink back into your old ways. Be committed to growing and creating a life of long-term success.

What changes do you want to make personally?

_____

_____

_____

_____

_____

_____

_____

_____

_____

Why does change and commitment play an important part in helping you accomplishing your goals?

_____

_____

_____

_____

_____

_____

On a scale of 1 to 10 how committed are you to accomplishing your goals and creating the life you want to live? Explain. Ten being the highest level of commitment

_____

_____

_____

_____

_____

_____

## SOMETIMES YOU JUST HAVE TO FIGURE IT OUT AS YOU GO

Each time you successfully complete a step toward your goal, you boost your confidence. With each step, you are clearing your path and making room for growth. Remember, it is ok to take the next step while feeling afraid. The benefits will far outweigh the temporary jitters. You make not have every detail figured out, but don't allow that to keep you from moving forward. When you make a move despite fear, doubt and insecurity, you are dismissing self-defeating thoughts, emotions and taking responsibility for the outcome of your life. As you continue the pattern of boldly moving forward in the face of fear, you are essentially throwing those negative feelings and thoughts away, and replacing them with courage. Now you are on your way to living a fearless life. You are clear about who you are and confident about what you want.

Reflect on your C.O.R.E. Motivators–Keep them in front of you at all times.

What's your motivation to keep going?

_____

_____

_____

_____

Ask yourself, what was your purpose for starting this journey?

_____

_____

_____

_____

_____

_____

_____

Avoid looking back—Keep your gaze straight ahead.

Why is it important to continue looking forward?

_____

_____

_____

_____

_____

Be Your Biggest Cheerleader.

What do you have to cheer about?

_____

_____

_____

_____

_____

What qualities and strengths do you need to help propel you forward?

_____

_____

_____

_____

_____

Revisit goals often. Write them down

How would you feel if you didn't accomplish your goal? Why?

_____

_____

_____

_____

_____

How would you feel if you achieved your goals? Why?

_____

_____

_____

_____

_____

KEEP YOUR MOMENTUM GOING, STAY FOCUSED, KEEP
YOUR GOAL IN SIGHT, KEEP MOVING AND FIGURE IT OUT

## THIS IS NOT A ONE-TIME FIX

You have to routinely throw away mental garbage just as you do physical garbage otherwise fear, doubt and insecurity will resurface—pile up and block your path. The key is to regularly throw away the mental garbage as you do your physical garbage. Throw it away and do not look back. When you treat mental garbage as physical garbage it will make it easier to let go of your fears and to toss doubts and insecurities away. You will be able to keep on going because you are in control of your feelings and thoughts. You will come to realize that certain people's perceptions just don't matter. You will become better at identifying what you need to keep and what you need to throw away.

At times our imperfect state may give rise to:

Fear

Doubt

Insecurity

Anger

Pride

Blame

You have to realize that these things do not serve your purpose. You know what you want out of life, refuse to allow anything or anyone to stand in your way. It takes discipline to be successful. Be proactive in sticking to a routine that keeps your mental space organized and clear.

**Do not allow garbage to clutter your mind—your life!**

## HAVE GOALS

Expect to win. Your goals can easily be crowded out by everyday life. Your mind is constantly going, going and going. When you take a moment to write down your goals, your mind shifts and slows down. When you give yourself time to process things and truly see your vision, you are creating space to bring your ideas, your goals to life.

You have to set goals in order to advance. Setting goals helps you to map out your life's plan. Goals help you to get your life organized and creates structure. Setting goals can give you insight as to whether or not you are going in the right direction. Writing down your goals in addition to a detail plan for achieving your vision will  mininize distractions and keep you focused. Goals provide a map outlining your destination for the day, the week, the month, the year, the next five years. You have to know where you are going in order to get there!

### DO YOU WRITE DOWN YOUR IDEAS, YOUR GOALS?

With so much going on in our lives work, school, finances, family, unexpected events, etc., things get lost in the shuffle. You only have to make one adjustment and that is to write your goals and ideas down.  Start a journal.  I know you have heard this numerous times, but it works.  It helps you to be present with your ideas rather than seeing them from a distant. You do not want your ideas, your goals to become fleeting thoughts that get pushed aside, buried under the daily challenges of life. Writing down your goals help you plan your moves to be successful in life.

SET GOALS, yes WRITE THEM DOWN. Write down specific steps you are going to take to reach your goals.

Next, TAKE ACTION, but not blindly, with each goal that you set out to achieve, do your research so that you are proceeding with knowledge rather than assumptions.

Make Things Happen. Surround yourself with people who have similar goals. If you don't know anyone personally who has the same goal, find stories about individuals who share similar goals. Read about their success stories.

## BLOCK OUT THOSE WHO DOUBT YOU

Journaling helps you keep your goals in focus and create a vision for your life. Writing down your goals, thoughts, feelings, failures, successes and past experiences can be a real eye opener. Writing helps you to see whether you are on the right path allowing you to refer back to your goals as often as you like and make adjustments along the way. I encourage you to keep two journals. One for your garbage, the thoughts you need to get rid of and one for self-discovery, leading you to find your true story.

It is important to purposefully pursue your goals, get into motion, and take action. Every waking moment is an opportunity to take a step toward your goals.

Do not look away from your goals. The moment you look away, obstacles will stand taller than life itself and your goals will begin to fade because they will seem impossible to reach.

Having goals add meaning and purpose to your life. Goals give you something to strive for and they help keep the GARBAGEOUT of your life.

**G**arbageOut

**O**pportunity

**A**chieve

**L**ife

**S**ucceed

Getting the **GARBAGEOUT** opens up the door of **OPPORTUNITY** for you to **ACHIEVE** your goals giving you **LIFE** and the courage to **SUCCEED**

## P.U.S.H

Your mood may be dreary, you feel tired, you don't feel like you can go on—at this time muster up the strength to keep pushing

P.U.S.H. Push until something happens. Face your fears head on; push through the uncomfortable phases of life. When you turn the corner and things start to happen, your mood will begin to lift; your outlook on life will change. Keep pushing! Give it all you got, do not turn around. Keep pressing forward. You are made to endure life's trials. Life is challenging you to grow.

What challenges are you facing right now?

_____

_____

_____

_____

_____

_____

_____

Why is it important to keep pushing forward and not give up despite challenges you are facing? What would be the benefit?

_____

_____

_____

_____

_____

How can you grow from life's challenges?

_____

_____

_____

_____

_____

_____

## JUST MAKE IT HAPPEN

Do what it takes to be the person you want to be. You are not helpless, however, listening to negative thoughts and perceptions of others can make you feel that way. You are much bigger than thoughts that try to crowd out your potential. The perception of others is not your reality so let them think what they like; their approval is not needed.

Once you understand that this is your life, do not allow your attention to be diverted. Some of you may feel that you are not in control. You may feel that your thoughts are all over the place. You can't focus, you are anxious, you feel overwhelmed. You just don't see a way out.

## How to Gain Control and Make Things Happen in Your Life

TAKE A CHANCE ON YOU. This says so much about your character, your strength, your drive and your will to succeed.

IDENTIFY YOUR CORE MOTIVATORS. You have to have something or someone in your life that motivates you from the core, from the depth of your very being, giving you that extra push to keep going, to remind you why you started on this journey in the first place. Always be mindful that your number one motivator should be you, you hold the key to your success.

ONE STEP AT A TIME. A new beginning starts with one step then another. Never stand still.

MAKE MISTAKES. Making mistakes are part of the process. No imperfect human being has lived a life free of mistakes. You can't let past mistakes stop you from moving forward with life. Learn from your mistakes and see how you can do things better in the future.

TAKE RESPONSIBILITY. Take time to determine where you went wrong and then accept that you are not perfect. Your path will become clearer when you focus on the solution rather than the problem.

NEVER STOP. Stay in pursuit of your goal until you have accomplished what you have set out to do. Keep it moving!

BELIEVE IN YOURSELF. When you trust in the power that has been given to you, you believe that you are entitled to success, you commit to doing what is necessary to reach your goals. Belief in yourself is always going to be a key component in accomplishing your goals. When you believe in yourself you are not going to allow self-defeating thoughts to linger. You are going to dismiss them quickly and focus on thoughts that will serve you, enabling you to embrace your power and live your life with courage, boldness and fearlessness.

**Everything starts and ends with your mental perception of self. Be clear and confident about what you want and just make it happen.**

*If your life is a story, who is the author—YOU*

*You can change your story anytime you want*

## LIFE WAITS FOR NO ONE

Life will continue to go on whether you choose to be an active participant or not. It is your choice. You have a choice either to sit on the sideline and be a spectator or you can play the game and make choices that will determine your life course, instead of allowing someone else to choose for you. There will be times when you win and there will be times when you lose. The most important factor is that you choose to be a participant. Being in the game helps you sharpen your decision making skills, so that you can make choices that will help you win more than you lose.

In life you have to continue to focus and refocus. It is part of the process of getting the garbage out. This may sound like work because it is work. You are in training. Mentally, you are dumping years and years of garbage, bad thoughts and habits that have been etched in your mind. Now, you are revising the way you think and behave. The more you put forth effort to form better habits the easier it becomes. You have to dump and leave the old way of thinking, the old habits, which have no value.

*To make room for a new way of thinking, you must let something go and develop new habits that will keep your mind mentally clean and take your game to the next level*

Forming new habits takes time. It will require patience. Be persistent about removing the garbage from your life. Don't live your life based on regrets. Regrets cloud your mind, consume your thinking, take up your time and energy and before you know it, not only have you spent a day thinking and meditating on regrets, you have spent a lifetime wishing you would have done things differently. Do not let your life pass you by. Decide to be happy now. Stop waiting for that perfect moment to truly start living your life. Live in the present, make plays that matter, be in the game. Life waits for no one. Do not allow your thoughts to constantly shift back to *I* should have done this, replaying it over and over in your mind. These thoughts come from a place of self-defeat, you are positioning yourself to lose. Instead of saying, "If only I would have done this, say, I am going to look at my options and see how I can move forward from this by doing something different." This statement is coming from a place of power. This puts you in control of the game and your life.

When you make the shift, you have to understand that there is a responsibility that comes with maintaining your position. A routine has to be put in place to keep your path clear to allow you to continue moving forward. If you make the shift and do nothing to maintain your position or continue growing, you will begin to shift backwards and revert back to your old way of thinking and doing things. There has to be a system in place.

Do you choose to sit on the sideline and be a spectator or do you choose to play in the game? Why?

_____

_____

_____

_____

_____

What are you determined to do differently in life, to make your life better?

_____

_____

_____

_____

_____

_____

How can you sharpen your decision-making skills?

_____

_____

_____

_____

_____

_____

_____

How will you prepare yourself to win more than you lose?

_____

_____

_____

_____

_____

_____

_____

_____

_____

_____

**Remember, life waits for no one. We live in motion, not standing still, make the choice to participate in your life, be in the game to win.**

## MEDITATION
## KEY TO FINDING YOUR WAY

Do not allow life to defeat you, destroy you, tear you down or stomp you into the ground. GET UP and FIGHT for your life. Stand up and say I am here, what am I supposed to do? Then sit still; relinquish the fear, anger, resentfulness, doubt, insecurity and disappointment. Do not make time for garbage in your life; meditate on letting go.

Give yourself time to sit still for at least for five minutes a day. Mediate on bringing peace into your life and accomplishing your goals. Mentally walk through the details of each step you are going to take and see yourself hitting your target. Mediate on the good things that have happened in your life, the lessons you have learned. Meditate on the wonderful gift of life. Make sure gratitude is a part of your meditation. Once you feel the power of the garbage you have accumulated over the years start to weaken, you will begin to feel the weight lifting. The answers will start to come because you are letting go of the thoughts that are contaminating your mind. You are freeing up space to grow, to be better and to be present.

You are reshaping your thoughts and training your mind to focus. Most importantly, you are taking control of your life. Now take action. Work in harmony with your thoughts and watch the connection begin to take place.

Stillness should be a regular part of your daily routine; start with five minute intervals then gradually increase the time you mediate. Mediation keeps you centered, alert and aware of your surroundings. When you start feeling heavy, weighed down stop and pause for a moment to clear your mind to reflect on goodness, kindness, things that will uplift you and help you remain in control. Make mediation a practice even when things are going well and you are feeling light as a feather. This will help keep your mental space free of garbage, clearing a path so that you can find your way even through challenging situation.

Is your life worth fighting for? Why?

_____

_____

_____

_____

_____

What do you appreciate most about life? What uplifts you, brings you joy?

_____

_____

_____

_____

_____

_____

_____

How can meditation play a role in harmonizing your thoughts and actions?

_____

_____

_____

_____

_____

_____

What is the benefit of reshaping your thoughts?

_____

_____

_____

_____

_____

_____

## BE MINDFUL

*Being mindful moves you to be appreciative and the more you show appreciation, the more it extends to other parts of your life: family, financial, relationships and career*

Expressing your appreciation to others shifts your focus away from discontentment, making room for you to be happy. In order to go on when you are having a bad day, week, month or even year, be thankful that you have a new day to strive to be the best that you can be.

*Being mindful means you are appreciative of each day. You show this by taking notice of things big and small*

Take the sun for instance: it is big yet appears to be very small. It gives off light to the whole world, but yet it still shines on you, sustaining your life. Its power is one that can be imitated. You will reap powerful results and do big things by taking small steps, combined with a clear vision, an action plan and the determination to keep moving forward. The sun lights up your day giving you the inspiration to get out of bed and get moving. The full light of day gives you the opportunity to get things done. It does not force you, it does not pressure you to do anything, but it still shines for you, guiding you and encouraging you to shine, so be mindful and seize the day.

When you are mindful you do not make room for nonsense, you do not make room for unnecessary distractions, when the unexpected happens you are able to take the necessary steps and take care of your business—your life is your business.

When you truly understand that life will have its ups and downs, you are able to respond with wisdom. Wisdom is the ability to use insight and discernment to make informed decisions. Wisdom is also knowing that through faith, you have the strength to get through anything, however, first, your faith has to be built and maintained to strengthen you to withstand the storm when it comes.

Just imagine a tornado coming through your life, wreaking havoc, destroying everything in its path. Picture in your mind the mental damage that it could cause—confusion, immense fear, anger, uncontrollable tears. You wander, "why is this happening to me?" The stress and mental garbage begins to mount. It is just too overwhelming: you lost your business, your home, sentimental keepsakes, your car—you cannot handle it, so you think.

Majority of us will not experience our lives crashing down all at once, but for some it has and we can learn a lesson from their experience. Many of you have seen news reports where a person has lost everything due to a natural disaster, quite a number of them respond when being interviewed, "I am happy, I have my life." You build strength by being appreciative of each day that light shines on you.

## Mindfulness brings about appreciation for life
## be mindful, be thankful

What do you appreciate about life? Now, what do you appreciate about your life?

## THE ROAD NEVER ENDS

The road never ends
Somewhere along the way, encounters with obstacles made you
stumble
Disappointments shock
Challenges paralyze your every move
You experience loneliness along your journey
You have come to a dead end; you have no idea which way to go
Fear travels alongside you as you travel an unknown path
Self-doubt tripped you causing you to fall
You came to a roadblock and you turned around
You searched for a new path, but you gave up to easily
Traveling alone, you became afraid
Self-destruction begin to speak, this is not worth it
I should have just stayed home
Wary, tired, overwhelmed you feel
You have hit another roadblock, but the road never ends
The journey seems too long, too rugged
Focus just a little to see through the cloud
Your vision is there just hidden by fear you meet along the way
Just think how far you have come and the lessons you have
learned
A few more steps, don't stop to soon, the opportunity is there
The road never ends


~P. Ashworth

## WHERE'S YOUR FOCUS

Where you place your focus will determine the energy you generate in your life, whether the energy you are drawing is negative or positive. Whether or not you look forward to getting up in the morning. If you are excited about taking on the day, where you place your focus will play a major role in having a successful day—a successful life.

Your ability to focus will depend largely on the thoughts that you hold onto. Are your thoughts empowering you or suppressing you? There is so much you can focus your attention on in a positive way. It is truly a waste of time to focus on anything that does not contribute to your growth as a person.

*FOCUS ON LEARNING, GROWING AND HELPING OTHERS*

Focus in on life, look at the details of your life. Be clear about where you are in your life right now.

**Have your recent choices moved you closer to accomplishing your goals or is it time to take a different path?**

Be clear about the path you are on, and if it is time to take a different path, do so. When you take an honest look at your life, and you feel something just isn't right, it usually isn't. Where your focus lies, will determine your life course. Pay attention, get focused; create a clear picture as to where you want to be in your life.

Are you focused on living a happier more successful life? Why is being happy and successful important to you?

_____

_____

_____

_____

_____

How do you feel about your personal life, right now? How can you make it better?

_____

_____

_____

_____

_____

_____

Are you happy with the direction your professional life is heading? Why or Why not. What would you change or keep the same?

_____

_____

_____

_____

_____

Write down specific steps you can take today to shift your focus to what really matters in your life?

_____

_____

_____

_____

_____

**LIVE A STORY YOU WOULD LOVE TO TELL**
**One of Courage, Boldness and Fearlessness**

~P. Ashworth

# CHAPTER FOUR

## RECYCLE THE LESSON

## LISTEN BEYOND THE NOISE

Life is teaching you, it is training you. Are you listening? Are you listening to what life is trying to teach you?

What is distracting you? Identify the garbage

What lessons are you missing in your experiences?

What are the benefits of listening?

You have to discipline yourself to listen—to listen beyond the noise and act with intention. When you listen intentionally, you are listening to learn, to find the lesson—to find your way. When you act with intention, you are acting to bring about a desired result. There is no confusion as to the direction you are heading.

As you learn to listen to the lessons life is trying to teach you, your state of awareness grows. Your decision-making skills become better, leading you to a life full of meaning and purpose.

### *DISCIPLINE YOURSELF TO LISTEN, TUNE INTO YOUR LIFE*

Many times people think of discipline as a bad thing, however the definition of discipline is to teach. Think of discipline as a way to discover your untapped assets, skills, talents and gift. Most importantly discipline yourself to find you. As you discipline yourself, you start to take note of your surroundings and recognize the need for change. Many times you miss the lesson because you are so busy paying attention to the garbage that is infiltrating your life. You miss the lesson over and over again. As a result, you keep going down the same path that you so desperately want to get off of.

Being busy does not necessarily mean being physically busy, you can be so consumed with the negative flow of thoughts that constantly race through your mind that you miss out on living life. Thoughts from the past, worries about the future—it is the continuous whirlwind of thoughts that drain your time and energy, keeping you spinning in every direction. It is impossible for you to focus. If there is no room to focus, most of your goals will become lost as they intermingle with your scattered thoughts and lose the power to survive. Life is about learning and growing. If you are not listening, you are missing the opportunity to learn and grow from your experiences, to become a better you.

There is a voice that doesn't use words, but it is trying to tell you something. Discipline yourself to pay attention—to listen!

## *LISTEN TO THE LESSON*

What did you learn? You cannot allow past mistakes to stop you from moving forward with your life. Learn from your mistakes and take notice of how you can do things better next time. Never stop until you have accomplished what you set out to do. Keep moving! No Excuses.

Often times it is easier to recall negative life experiences in great detail while our positive experiences are hidden away, minimized or even forgotten due to the overwhelming, lingering feelings of regret and disappointment—the noise that drowns out your inner spirit. The noise dominates your thinking and place a shadow over anything positive that may happen, creating a pattern of thinking that generates a mental roadblock of confinement. No matter your goal in life; listening to the noise prevents you from enjoying life.

When you experience a setback in life—loss of employment, financial issues—doubts and insecurities start to creep in. How in the world am I going to get out of this situation?

*Listening for Directions on How to*
*Move Forward Requires Awareness*

**"And your own ears will hear a word behind you saying, this is the way. Walk in it, in case you should go to the right or in case you should go to the left"**

**Isaiah 30:21**

Listen with the intent to acquire the wisdom to take appropriate action. Whether it is to stay on the same path or change directions. There is nothing wrong with taking another path as long as you don't quit. What you take away from your everyday life experiences can benefit you along your journey. Listen with intention, be alert.

The power of paying attention to the unspoken word leads to conscious listening. It reinforces the need to let go of fear, doubt, insecurity; the distractions that keep you from hearing clearly. It prevents mental garbage from building up and helps you discover your truth.

Your truth will be revealed to you as you listen and begin to grasp the true meaning of life. It is not about money or fame; it's about gaining peace, creating balance and gaining control over your thoughts and your life. As you begin to build your life on this new foundation, your growth will take you to a new level of consciousness; your awareness will be heightened.

To get to a new level of consciousness and develop a heightened sense of awareness, you have to let go of the fear, feelings of insecurity that take hold of your mind and nurture doubt. When you hold onto fear, doubt and insecurity, mental garbage builds stagnating your growth. This lowers your volume, distracting you from paying attention to what really matters. As mental garbage accumulates, the noise of your uncontrolled life increases.

Listening intentionally, acting with intention transforms and declutters your mind of garbage, freeing up space to grow and clearing a path that will allow you to move, giving you freedom to be in control of your life. Listening is a skill that can empower you. It can transform your life.

What I have come to learn is that when you are facing a challenge and feel like you are about to lose it, in that moment you must be still and listen. The stillness brings you back to your center, quiets the noise, bringing you to a peaceful place, preparing you to listen and to receive the lesson.

*Every challenge you face gives you the opportunity to learn and grow. It requires that you listen. Will you except the challenge?*

When you listen with the aim to learn, to become a better you and grow, you will be able to face life's challenges with wisdom. The wisdom to use insight and discernment to guide your life; the art of listening has to be cultivated. It takes effort to listen with the right ear because for so long you have been listening with a deceptive ear telling you that you are not worthy, smart enough, too busy, too old.

### The Right Ear vs. Deceptive Ear

The right ear tells you to think before you speak or respond. The deceptive ear tells you to react immediately, even in anger. What you hear is determined by which ear you are using to listen. For instance, listening with the deceptive ear causes discouragement, fear, anger, regret and the build up of mental garbage. Listening with right ear propels you forward, knocks down barriers and clears your path of debris.

*Mastering the art of listening requires patience and practice, you have to be selective about what and who you listen to*

The deceptive ear hears things and compels you to act irrationally without thinking or seriously considering your next step. The deceptive ear listens to be a reactor, to allow fear, doubt and insecurity to set in. The mental garbage you have accumulated overtime takes over, causing you to listen defensively in readiness to attack.

The right ear listens to learn, improve oneself and to grow, opening up the way for inner peace. This allows you to response with wisdom. Listening for the lesson gives you the wisdom needed to move forward, clearing your mental path to focus on the solution rather than the problem.

## WHAT IS NOISE?

*Noise is anything that distracts you from hearing your truth. Noise drowns your true inner voice. The noise can be so loud that it puts up a sound barrier between you and the vision of what your life could be. The noise of mental garbage blurs your vision to the point where it is barely recognizable.*

Pay attention to how you listen. Listen to learn, listen to grow. Listen to learn more about yourself, listen to bring your vision into focus. Listening will prompt you to ask honest questions of yourself. Listen closely so that the lesson shines through and the true being of who you are opens up to you. As you work toward being in a state of awareness, being present and listening with the right ear; your true identity will be revealed to you and then it is up to you to take action!

## LIFE STRUGGLES WILL COME

There will be times when you will stumble, you may even fall, be determined to get back up, over and over again. Choose not to be the victim. Sometimes things can happen to give you a wakeup call. Sometimes the fall can knock you flat on your behind. It doesn't mean you give up; it means you put up a fight.

It takes intentional effort to become the person you want to be; it is not going to happen automatically. You have to begin taking steps in the direction of your goals, positioning yourself to seize the opportunity.

As you find your truth, live your truth; life challenges will not be such an overwhelming force in your life. When you find your place, you will increase your ability to walk through challenges with grace, dealing with each situation as it comes, looking at the solution instead of the storm, knowing that it too shall pass. If you were to focus your attention on the storm, the longer it would stay, focusing your attention on the solution quiets the internal storm going on inside you. There will be no internal struggle going on without your permission.

Chaos maybe going on around you, but it is not going on within you. You are in a position to direct your attention to the area most needed and proceed to handle the situation with confidence and courage. You are in control of the situation the situation is not in control of you. The more you handle life challenges in this way; you will harness your power, instead of wasting your precious resources in a non-productive way. Reserving your power, energy and time to focus your attention where it really matters.

*Life's struggles will come; challenge yourself to overcome them and move on*

123

## FOCUSING ON PAST MISTAKES, LIMITS FUTURE OPPORTUNITIES

Regret of past mistakes weigh you down, attack your spirit, your very being and your drive to keep going. Dwelling on past mistakes is a sign that you need to let it go. The reoccurrence of thoughts of past mistakes also indicate that your thoughts of the past, rather than thoughts of the present, are controlling your life. You are being controlled by thoughts of events that have already occurred, think about that; the self-defeating thoughts are shaping your life, placing limits on your future and blocking the path of opportunity.

To prevent making the same mistake in the future, find the lesson in the experience. When a similar situation presents itself,think about the lesson you have learned. How have you grown from the experience? Remember mistakes happen. They are part of the journey.

Next time, just do things differently to avoid repeating the same mistake. It is rare that anyone succeeds the first time. With each mistake you make you are getting closer to your goal. You are not tripping over the same debris, you have moved beyond that experience and taken the lesson and used your lessons to clear your path.

Planning ahead opens your path to opportunity and decreases the likelihood of repeating mistakes; when a mistake does happen, consider it a stepping stone to get to the next level of you life.

*Grow and learn from mistakes*
*Stay optimistic and keep on stepping*

## Mistakes are a part of the learning process:

- Identify mistakes and avoid repeating them
- Planning ahead, prepares you for opportunity
- Use mistakes as stepping stones

When you view mistakes as a way to get to know yourself better, discover your strengths, build your confidence—you remove the limits placed on your life. You come to realize that if you do XYZ, this will be the outcome. If an undesired outcome results, review your plan and revise it. Reflect on the decisions that lead you to making the mistake. Make a mental note as to why the mistake occurred, better yet; write it down. Now think about what you can do to correct the mistake. Think about your options and plan your next step. You are being proactive; you are putting stepping stones in place to get to the other side. See mistakes as a way to learn to do something better. Continue this process and as time goes on, fewer mistakes will surface because you no longer view your mistakes as something negative, but as a way to learn and improve your life. Making mistakes helps you to grow when you view them properly.

Mistakes will happen, just get back up; you are not perfect.

*One wise Proverbs says, "even if a good person falls seven times, he/she will get back up."*

*Proverbs 24:16*

**RISE AND CONTINUE YOUR JOURNEY**

What are some mistakes you have made in the past that are still difficult for you to let go?

_____

_____

_____

_____

_____

Think about the lessons you can learn from your mistakes. Choose to hold onto the lesson, let the mistake go.

Now how can you start applying these lessons in your life today?

_____

_____

_____

_____

_____

_____

## TALK WITH FEAR, WALK WITH FEAR
## CHALLENGE FEAR AND GROW

### Fear Exists for Two Reasons

**TO WARN YOU OF DANGER** if fear sends out a feeling of uneasiness or tension, you need to evaluate those feelings. Are the feelings truly valid? We all have seen movies where a person hesitates to open a door or enter a house because of the fear of what maybe on the other side. In this situation you need to listen to fear.

**TO SEND A SIGNAL WHEN YOU ARE GOING IN AN UNFAMILAR DIRECTION.** This is when you need to quiet your fear and listen for guidance. It is all about being in control and not allowing fear to control you.

Fear can be a protection telling you not to go in a certain direction because you sense danger ahead. Fear can also arise because you are taking a different path or going in an unfamiliar direction. This sets off an internal alarm because you are pushing new boundaries and testing uncharted waters, so I encourage you to walk with fear, talk with fear, challenge fear and determine whether you should be truly afraid or not.

**Listen to distinguish between fear that presents a sign of real danger and fear that challenges you to change, grow or make a shift in your life**

For instance, if your car breaks down in the middle of the night, you are not too far from home, you decide to walk. You can either choose to take a shortcut down a dimly lit street that is usually abandoned this time of night or fear may tell you to take the long way around in an area that is well lit.

### WHAT DO YOU DO?

You listen to fear and take the street that is well lit

On the other hand, when fear is trying to box you in, daring you to step outside the box, you should go against fear because the box is only an illusion.

*The only box that exist is the internal box that you create*

Once you accept that fear is just an emotion that warns you of impending danger or gives you a signal that you are going in an unfamiliar direction, you can make the choice to embrace fear or let it go.

*When fear does not present a true danger you can make the decision to take a step forward, believing that nothing will stand in your way*

Walk with fear, talk to fear, challenge fear because it will always try to resurface; whatever you do, do not allow fear to back you in a corner. Usually people aren't afraid of what has already happen, they are usually afraid of what is going to happen in the future. Why fear something that hasn't even happen yet? Decide now to replace fear with optimism and look to the future with a positive outlook. Do not allow fear to rule your life. There is a difference between feeling the emotion of fear and giving into it. Lesson learned, living beyond fear leads to freedom!

## YOU HOLD THE POWER

You hold the power to determine what dominates your thinking. When garbage tries to creep into your mind, telling you what you can't do? Firmly reply, "YES, I CAN. No one will listen to you—YES, THEY WILL. That's not a good idea. Say to yourself, I WILL NOT KNOW IF I DON'T TRY." Continue this internal dialogue until the positive thoughts dominate the conversation. Work on something everyday to improve yourself, to build your confidence, to increase your strength.

What you think you will live and what you live you will be. There is no way around it. What you think about will always surface in your physical life. The mental garbage that has been accumulating in your mind over the years, clouds your vision, causing you to lose sight of who you are. It causes distractions that prevent you from living a happy, meaningful life. The things you think about will either move you closer to living your best life or push you further back. If you allow fear, insecurity and doubt to dominate your thinking, they will trap you, causing you to place limits on what you can accomplish, interfering with your whole life. These self-defeating thoughts will continue to interrupt your life until you let them go. Be mindful of the things you allow into your life whether through television, music or people. They all affect your thinking and actions.

You will have bad experiences in life, wallowing in sorrow and self-pity gets you nowhere.

*Self-pity can be defined as excessive, self-absorbed*
*unhappiness over one's troubles*

Your circumstances can change; your attitude makes all the difference. Your thoughts can empower you to change your attitude and your situation. Be determined to rise above the walls of self-pity and get things done. Instead of complaining and holding onto yesterday's problem, get to work on creating the life you desire to live today. Through conscious thought you can increase your energy level, and live a more productive and happier life. Your conscious thoughts are the driving force behind your mood and your success at work and in life.

*Don't allow yourself to be a victim of life*
*Life happens to all of us*

You can choose to create a new beginning or be absorbed in self-pity, which keeps you focused on the pain, the hurt and the unfairness of life. Life can be unfair sometimes, but there are also many opportunities to experience the fairness and goodness in life.

## CHOOSE TO SEE THE GOOD

The good lifts your spirits to new heights, above the walls of self-pity. The lesson will help you to regain focus. Be determined to focus in on life's opportunities that allow you to learn, grow and build strong dependable relationships.

Never stay down for the count. There will be times when you will fall down and you may even need to cry, however, there comes a time when you have to wipe away the tears and let go. Muster up the strength to firmly plant your feet for the fight that lies ahead. Fight to get to a better life, fight until the very end. You hold the power to create the life you want to live.

## 7 STEPS TO COMPLETENESS

*We all want to feel complete, to get to a place where you feel completely at peace with yourself a merger has to take place*

You first have to work on what is going on mentally. Your mental state is the driving force behind your physical state. Your mental state, the way you think. The way you process information has a direct effect on your emotions, your response to life; the actions you choose to take or not to take.

It will take effort on your part to get to a state of completeness. It starts with letting go of the garbage. Mental garbage maybe one of the hardest things to throw away; reoccurring thoughts that tear you down, minimize your existence, block your path—have to go! You have to be honest with yourself and do the work. Let's take a look at seven steps that will help you get on the path to feeling complete and at peace with who you are.

## 7 STEPS TO COMPLETENESS

## 1. Ask Honest Questions and Give Honest Answers

Asking questions opens doors. Ask yourself honest questions and give honest answers: what, when, how, where and why. Example, what is this experience trying to teach me? How can I move forward in my life? Where is this journey leading me? Why do I feeling stuck? When will my life change for the better? Internalize the question, sit still, mediate on the question; next listen for an honest answer. When answering honestly you will be given insight as to things you need to let go, whether you should stay on the same path or change directions as well as areas in your life where you need to make improvements. The next step is to respond to the question through action.

You received the answer, now you have to act. There has to be a merger of your thoughts and actions—your thoughts being your mental state and your actions being your physical state. There has to be harmony between your mental and physical state before you can experience harmony and peace in your life—completeness

## 2. Build Self-Worth, Walk the Talk

Know your worth as a person; stand in your power: Start by identifying your strengths, acknowledge them and accept them. You gain your power from the strength you possess or acquire.

When you set a goal, do everything in your power to achieve it. When you achieve your goals you are building your self-worth, making inroads to clearing your mental path of garbage. Each time you accomplished a goal you walk taller, with a stride that is confident, bold and unstoppable. You hold your head a little higher, not trembling at fear. You are building a foundation that is unshakable.

List your strengths, then list a piece of garbage that you are going to throw away.

**Value/Strength**

_____

_____

_____

## Garbage/Weakness

_____

_____

_____

_____

_____

Identifying your strengths will help you to see your value and bring your strengths to the forefront of your mind, your life. You have the power to pull yourself up, to change your life. Use your power to save yourself and stop waving the white flag of distress waiting for someone else to come save you.

Truly believing that you have the power to move mountains will enable you to move anything blocking your path. Harness your power, know your worth and let go of anything that is draining your strength, your value. Use your power confidently; it increases your value.

When garbage tries to resurface, zap it with your power—your strength. Tell fear to take a back seat. Now let your actions prove to fear who's in control, value yourself enough to stand up for you!

Your goal should be to become better than you were yesterday; with each step toss fear, doubt and any insecurity in the garbage can where they belong. With each courageous step you take you are gaining power, building your strength and increasing your value—your self-worth.

## 3. Mental Exercise

Exercise your mind. Mental exercise is necessary to retrain your thinking; use affirmations and meditation to counteract the garbage that continuously tries to creep into your life.

You are not taught to think negatively, you are born with an inclination to lean toward negativity. You have to be trained to have a positive line of thought. It does not happen naturally. This is why training is so vital even for adults. The training process is about learning and growing, it never ends so embrace it, love it because you will emerge a better, wiser and stronger person.

Mental Exercise: Repeat Affirmations

The thoughts you think throughout the day create your reality. Using affirmations will help you create the life you want to live. Affirmations put you in control of your thoughts. Choosing to use words that uplift you throughout the day significantly reduces the risk of negativity controlling your life. This is the beginning of developing a connection between you and your inner world, merging the two together. This is the connection that will start to stir in you the desire to do something about achieving your goals.

When you routinely use affirmations you will notice the flow of your life changing; you attract positive energy into your life; putting you in a positive state of mind.

Affirmations uplift, strengthens your resolve to stay the course, builds your faith, gives you reassurance, mental clarity of your worth and positions you to be the best person you can be. Now create that person by bringing the person you are aspiring to be into the present.

Mental Exercise: Meditation

Meditation helps you get to a place of awareness. Awareness of how your thoughts affect your actions, how your actions affect your life; I cannot stress awareness enough. If you are not conscious of your thoughts, conscious of who you are, someone else is determining your thoughts and controlling your life.

Mediation is the gift of stillness opening a way for you to organize your thoughts and feelings, so that life can speak to you. Mediation grounds you, brings you to a place where you can be at peace, centered, focused, determined and open to accept the changes life brings.

## 4. Physical Exercise

Exercise your body. Physical exercise revitalizes your mind, body and spirit, giving you a threefold benefit. Your mind gets refreshed, your body gets toned and your spirit gets lifted. As you are exercising you are breathing in more oxygen, blood is pumping to your brain creating space for clarity and organization of your thoughts. Your body is responding to the physical work you are putting in and your mind is being refreshed, your spirit is being rejuvenated, you just feel good about yourself and reap the benefits of looking good as well.

## 5. Reflect on Life Lessons

Ask yourself, "What have I learned? When you take away the lesson you are armed with the tools to create success in your life. You avoid making the same mistakes over and over again. Lessons build you up making you stronger and confident about the next bold move you should take. Seek to grow from life lessons.

## 6. Develop Strong Reasoning Skills

Think things through; ask yourself, "How will this decision impact my life?"

*How to develop strong reasoning skill*

Look at the pros and cons

Visualize the big picture. See yourself accomplishing your goals and reaping the benefits of your work.

Stimulate your mind through regular exercise, reading, eating a healthy diet, learn something new, sharing your ideas and stepping outside your norm.

When making a decision think about the worst and best case scenario, then think about what will most likely happen.

Avoid irrational thinking, being stressed or angry can bring about irrational thinking, which could prompt you to make decision you would not otherwise make if you were calm and had the opportunity to think things through. Give yourself time to calm down before making a decision. If you have to make a decision immediately step away for a moment gather yourself weigh the pros and cons and think about the outcome that you want.

**Don't over think the situation, sometimes we can over think things and make matters worse. Over thinking interferes with your reasoning ability.**

*Be consistent*: develop a systematic way of solving problems

- Identify the problem

- Brainstorm at least three solutions when a problem arises

- Choose the best solution

- Take Action

*When you make good decisions you feel good about yourself*

## 7. Keep a Journal

Write about your past, present and future. Put your thoughts and feelings on paper, get it out! Journaling helps you to expand and explore your thoughts, makes you aware of what is taking place in your life, it helps you to pay attention, to focus, to redirect your energy if necessary. Keeping a Journal connects you with your life, creating a mentality that is driven by purpose focused thinking. Writing helps you to keep your goals in sight at the same time creating a path for you to move forward.

When you began to write down your disappointments, fears, doubts and past failures, it opens up a way to free yourself. The process of writing down your thoughts, feelings and plans filters out mental garbage that blocks your path and hinders you from clearly seeing your vision.  When you free yourself of self-defeating thoughts, you will be amazed at how your thoughts begin to take shape and the new insight that begins to emerge bringing about a sense of peace and a feeling of completeness because you are gaining control of your life.

Bonus: Wear "InspireMe" Bracelets

During the process of creating the "GarbageOut" brand; writing the first book in the "GarbageOut" book series, designing products for the brand; I came up with the idea to design a bracelet that not only look good, but also has a purpose—to inspire, motivate and empower.

During the last phase stages of creating the "GarbageOut" Brand I designed my first "InspireMe" bracelet. I wore the *Stay Strong Signature bracelet* it gave me that extra boost of motivation to keep going. Each time I looked down I was reminder to stay strong to keep going. It was amazing how powerful I felt wearing the *Stay Strong Signature bracelet*. I believe that words are powerful and can change your life.

Take a look at the InspireMe Signature Collection at

www.garbageoutdaily.com

You will not want to leave home without it. Put a picture of you wearing your "InspireMe" bracelet on Instagram; let's keep inspiring one another.

Seven Steps to Completeness will put you on the path to living a meaningful life, merging your thoughts and actions, creating an inner harmony that propels you forward; with each step you are building the confidence needed to succeed in both your personal and professional life. When you implement these steps you will see a huge shift in your life.

*What steps will you start applying in your life immediately?*

GARBAGEOUT

## FOCUS ON WHAT REALLY MATTERS

It's not about what happened yesterday, a week ago, a month ago, a year ago, 5, 10, 15, 20 years ago. What can you change? Focus on today; let go of the hurt, the anger and the blame. At the end of each day let go of the daily pressures of life, whether big or small. Take away the lesson rather than the disappointment, regret and fear from life experiences. As you began to focus on what really matters throughout the day, you will start to live your life in a more proactive and positive way, driven by thoughts that empower and uplift. The energy from living a proactive and positive life gradually shifts your thoughts, retrains your mind and builds your strength from the inside, out.

Everyday you have the opportunity to learn something new or to have a new experience. Often times these opportunities and experiences present themselves quite frequently, but you allow your mind to focus on negative thinking which produces garbage that blocks you from truly enjoying your life, preventing you from growing and learning more about you.

**You have to be in the right frame of mind to receive and recognize the true meaning of life**

Filter out the garbage that is holding you back from embracing the present moments. Thoughts that bring about feelings of worthlessness, anger and depression; zap your energy. Replace toxic thoughts with thoughts that refresh, motivate, energize, give you hope, courage and a new leash on life.

139

Keeping your eyes open for moments that add meaning and purpose to your life. As you begin to focus on what really matters; de-cluttering of your mental garbage starts to take place, clearing your path making room for new experiences and a better life.

You have to look at what is truly important to you to even begin to make sense of your life. Take an honest look at what is important to you and start throwing out the things that are nonessential.

**Ask yourself:**

What is important?

What really matters to me?

What moments can I take away from everyday experiences that will help me to grow, prosper and be better than I was yesterday?

## Focus on what really matters in your life!

## PAY ATTENTION

People, places, career choices, what makes you happy, what makes you sad, your eating habits, financial decisions and the steps you should take to accomplish your goals. Are you going in the right direction. Live your life intentionally! Pay Attention to what is going on around you.

### Are You Making Good Decisions in Your Life?

Opening your eyes to the truth reveals whether or not you are paying attention and being honest with yourself. When you act on truth, you will begin to see the results. If you refuse to pay attention and grasp the lesson you will remain in the same space.

### Nothing Will Change Until You Do!

Are the people you are surrounding yourself with making a positive or negative impact on your life? Explain

_____

_____

_____

_____

*Lesson:* Association Matters

Think about the people you socialize with on a regular bases, write a description of each relationship, indicate whether they are affecting your life positively or negatively

Can you make these relationship better or do you need to let them go. The choice is yours. Be honest with yourself it will be a difficult choice. Every relationship is not a good or health relationship.

Are you happy with your career choice? Why or Why Not? Explain.

_____

_____

_____

_____

Have your financial decisions put you in a better position in life or have your financial decisions been detrimental to your livelihood. How can you turn things around?

_____

_____

_____

_____

Are your eating habits contributing to a better quality of life? Why is it important to make better food choices?

_____

_____

_____

_____

_____

_____

_____

_____

_____

Pay attention to the decisions you make, how they impact your life and the final outcome of your decisions. Being present gives you the opportunity to evaluate your results, to determine whether or not you made a wise decision, to make adjustment where needed and to apply the lessons you have learned to start making better decision in your life.

**OPEN YOUR EYES, PAY ATTENTION**

## CARBON FOOTPRINT

What is your personal carbon footprint? The effects of pollution in the world is devastating. Efforts are being made to reduce the carbon footprint to make the world a better place to live. We are encouraged to use our resources wisely—water and electricity, to recycle and buy reusable goods. The choices you make may have a devastating effect on your life or they can help conserve your life and the lives of others.

### Five Ways to Leave a Positive Footprint:

- Live a conscious life, make conscious decisions
- Remember that first impressions matter so be prepared
- Embrace your power, but know when to conserve it
- Encourage others, give a positive word
- Decide to respond, not to react

Footprints leave an impression of who you are. What does your footprint say about you?

### Choose to be empowered and to empower others:

What are you doing to make yourself better?

What is your effect on the world and others around you?

What does your reflection say about you?

What footprint are you leaving?

Leave a footprint that shows that you are conscious of the decisions you make in life, business and relationships.

You hold the power to make choices that will affect your life and the lives of others in a positive way.

## RECYCLE THE LESSON

Learn from past mistakes, recycle the lessons to make better decisions in the future and throw away the rest.

## REUSABLE GOOD

*Knowledge* Learn from others, people are usually willing to share their knowledge. Do your own research, read and learn as much as you can. Knowledge is always reusable.

*Skills and Talents* You have learned new skills and enhanced your talents from previous jobs. Evaluate your skills and talents, put them to use to accomplish your personal goals.

## USE YOUR TIME, ENERGY AND RESOURCES WISELY

You have to discipline your mind to be disciplined about your time and resources. Use your time, energy and resources where they will serve you the most. Don't be wasteful.

Evaluate your carbon footprint from 1 to 10. Rate yourself a 10 if you are recycling life lessons from your experiences and reusing your goods: knowledge, skills, talents, time, energy and resources wisely. Most of us need to make some improvement within one or more areas in our lives.

How do you plan on improving your personal carbon footprint?

_____

_____

_____

_____

_____

_____

_____

_____

_____

**Why do you Keep Things you do not Want
and Hold onto Things you do not Need**
*KEEP ONLY WHAT WILL SERVE YOUR PURPOSE*

## BREAKDOWN
## GIVE UP OR USE THE LESSON

You can choose to breakdown, give up or use the lesson learned in life to overcome or cope with life challenges.

### PREPARE FOR THE CHALLENGE—USE THE LESSON

Use the lesson from past experiences to clear out the garbage, so you can think, think about challenges that may arise, apply the lessons learned. Ask yourself, how can I overcome this challenge? What are my options; identify solutions. Preparing for the challenge beforehand will help you to minimize the initial shock, regroup faster and respond to the situation instead of react. When you respond you are in control, when you react the situation is controlling you.

### GIVE UP

Let life challenges empower you, make you stronger, resilient and determined to stay the course. Giving up is never an option.

### AVOID A BREAKDOWN

Rest, think things through, regroup, talk to someone you can trust, focus on finding a solution now take positive action.

## IT IS NEVER TOO LATE TO START OVER

You can always get your life back on track. If you weren't happy with yesterday, try something different today. Don't allow yourself to be put in a negative state of awareness by being absorbed with thoughts about a particular event that you can't change.

**"When you know better you do better, now it is time to put what you have learned to work"**

The only way to shift your state of awareness is to pay attention to the lesson.

Ask yourself, what have I learned for yesterday's experience?

_____

_____

_____

_____

Focusing on the lesson will prevent garbage from piling up; this will help you to clear your path of mental garbage that has accumulated over the years.

## BENEFITS OF FOCUSING ON THE LESSON

You will have fewer stumbles and stagnated periods in your life. Notice I didn't say that this approach would completely prevent stumbles or negative situations from occurring, but rather it will greatly reduce the number of stumbles and falls you will have. Another benefit is that you are throwing away mental garbage, which allows you to think clearer and act intentionally. You will rebound quickly and remain focused on your goal.

When you learn the lesson you are learning about you and developing into a person who is aware, awake and alert. You are positioning yourself to have extraordinary experiences in life.

We spend a lot of time learning and studying about other people; turn your attention to yourself to create the life you want. Everyday gives you the opportunity to start over, to learn, to grow and discover you. It is never too late to find out how talented and gifted you are!

What qualities do you currently have that you absolutely love? Why?

_____

_____

_____

_____

_____

_____

What qualities would you like to cultivate? Why

_____

_____

_____

_____

_____

_____

_____

_____

Start cultivating qualities that will make you a better person; give yourself the attention you need to thrive. It's never too late to start over.

## RECYCLE

What do you do with garbage; throw it away? Think about throwing a ball, if you hand it to someone you still have your hand on it—you are not letting it go. You have to throw it, release the ball from your hand, but you still can run after the ball, it's your choice. Running after the balls means you still have work to do and that's ok we are all works in progress. The goal is to release and let go!

Now think about your mental garbage. When you keep holding onto garbage it is going to weigh you down; you are going to continuously smell the stench—throw the garbage away, close the door, let the garbage man pick it up and carry it away. Dump it and leave it wash your hands of it, do not run after it—release it and let it go.

Stop holding onto the mistake and hold onto the lesson. The lesson propels you forward, preparing you for the journey ahead, clearing the way for a better you to emerge. Let go of the garbage, recycle what is needed, the Lesson. Do not let anything come in between you living your life and becoming the best person you can possibly be. Do not settle.

Not a person, place, thing or thought should be given control over your life. You are worthy to be present in your life. You are worthy to enjoy precious moments in life, it's the moments that you cherish the most. Forgive yourself for past mistakes; let go of the burden, throw it away and relinquish the hold.

Select what will be useful on your journey and throw away the rest. You do not need the distractions or the extra weight. Holding onto something you don't need may tempt you to turn back to your old ways. Let go and recycle only what is needed for your journey.

# CHAPTER FIVE

# FREE UP SPACE TO GROW

## MAINTAIN YOUR STRENGTH

Do not allow your mind to dwell on things that will weaken you. You have to constantly root out destructive thoughts as soon as you de-value your self-worth, you lose sight of your vision. Then, the tendency to lean toward a negative reflection of yourself will return and the garbage will resurface. The state of your mental and physical well being is driven by the way you think, what you think about and how you think.

*Your thinking is a direct reflection of your life—finances, eating habits, career, family, spirituality and relationships*

You will transform your life when you transition your mind from a position of negativity to a position of awareness that drives positive thoughts and actions. The process is anything but simple; it really requires quite a bit of work to make the shift, to give your mind a makeover—to get the GarbageOut.

We live in a world where there is so much negativity around us: war, crime, injustice, hatred, glamorized violence. Even though these things may not be happening to you directly, they impact the way you think and feel about yourself. Just think, when you turn on the television, you invite all that negativity into your home. Not only do you have to be careful about the individuals you associate with, you have to be mindful of what you watch on television and the music you listen to—to safeguard your thinking. There is so much negativity in your midst, making it a constant struggle to prevent it from affecting your thoughts and draining your energy. You don't have to be apart of it. You don't have to involve yourself in all the drama. You have a choice and the way you think affects your choice.

What you feed your mind will determine your level of mental strength. If you want to train your mind and change your thinking, you have to change what you feed it.

What do you think about the most?

_____

_____

_____

_____

_____

Does your mind shift more toward negative or positive thinking? Why? What would be the benefit of having a positive mindset?

_____

_____

_____

_____

_____

How can you rise above life's disappointments, uncertainties, and distressing situations?

_____

_____

_____

_____

_____

_____

What specific things can you think about to help you build your mental strength?

_____

_____

_____

_____

_____

_____

## THE GIFTS WE TAKE FOR GRANTED

Friendship
Family
Other moment, other hour, other day
Peace of Mind
Strength to keep moving forward
Seeing the stars twinkle on a clear night
Freedom
Sandy beaches
Taste buds
A beautiful sunset
Fresh water to drink
Touch
Being able to see in color
Our beautiful minds
Thoughts
Music
Movement
Nature
Being able to hear different sounds and tones
Technology
The moon
Gravity
Imagination
Moments of Silence
Laughter

There is so much goodness you can fill your mind with. Find reasons to cherish your life, to feel good about yourself and to be thankful.

*Acknowledge your gifts and show gratitude*

What gifts do you appreciate the most? Why?

_____

_____

_____

_____

_____

_____

_____

_____

_____

Think about your gifts often, gratitude makes the mind and heart joyful. The more your thoughts are centered around your gift, the more clear and confident you will be. Live a life of gratitude.

## STILLNESS BRINGS ABOUT AWARENESS

It takes time to embrace stillness. It comes with appreciation of life. When you begin to see things in ways you never imagined, you are on your way to appreciating the gift of stillness. Your world will begin to open up, putting you in a state of awareness. Living in a state of awareness will put you on a whole different level. The things that most people overlook, take for granted, or see as unimportant, small or minor, you will see as the most important force in your life. Taking a walk, watching the sunset and eating a meal will not be the same anymore; your goals will be clear and you will be focused. Moments of stillness will become an essential part of your day.

To be honest it took me some time to acquire the appreciation for stillness. The first time I heard anyone speak about the topic of stillness was *Oprah*. The next day I went outside. I heard the birds singing, I gazed at the trees I didn't hear anything special. The birds were singing and the trees were standing. They didn't say anything to me.

It took years before I grasped the rich meaning of the connection of life's creations with my thoughts and with my very existence. As I begin to mediate things began to unfold, my appreciation deepened, my insight began to grow and my thoughts began to take shape. This came at a time when I was searching for meaning in my life. I was at a crossroads not knowing which way to go. There was something inside me begging to live, saying, don't let me die!

*I thought, "Now I understand what Oprah was talking about*
*when she explained her experience of walking among*
*the trees and listening."*

To hear your authentic voice you have to let go of the fear, insecurity and doubt. These feeling may linger at times, but do not allow them to linger too long and take control of your life. The emotions of life can cloud your vision, draining too much time and energy. Listen for the solution not all the negativity that comes along with challenges or unexpected situations. Know that you are more than capable to deal with anything that may come your way. You will not be given more than you can bear.

## BE STILL FOR A MOMENT
## LET THE ANSWERS COME

Plan ahead to manage mental garbage that comes your way everyday or it will overtake you, blocking out the voice of stillness. When you begin to understand who you are and stop being the person everyone else wants you to be, your authentic self has room to grow—to open up to you. Are you listening to your inner voice leading you to your passion, gift, talents and abilities? Embrace the stillness that surround you and listen!

It was stillness that lead me to accomplishing my goal of publishing my first book, "GarbageOut" and starting my own company. Stillness is a gift you should not take for granted.

## MOMENTARY AND LIGHT

*"For though the tribulation is momentary and light*
*it works out for us a glory that is of more and*
*more surpassing greatness and is everlasting"*

2 Corinthians 4:17

Do not allow tribulation to take away your joy. Find moments of joy even through the storm—until the clouds lift. Stay present in the moment so that the darkness does not overtake you. The sun pierces through, sustaining your every breath. Keep your face tilted to the rays of life. You are on a journey that only faith and courage will carry you through. View your trials as momentary and light and keep something far better in view.

Have faith, "faith is the assured expectation of the things hoped for, the evident demonstration of realities, though not seen."
~Hebrews 11:1

Even though things may not be as you envisioned them in this moment, have faith that everything will work out just as they should as you continue pressing forward doing the work that needs to be done.

## CREATING SPACE

The cycle of keeping and holding onto things flows over to every aspect of your life. Why do you keep things you do not want and hold onto things you do not need? You have to start letting go. Getting rid of things that add no value to your life frees up space and empowers you to open up your life to new possibilities.

So often, we forget about our cluttered mental space. For years, many of us have overlooked the importance of freeing our minds of self-destructive, self-defeating thoughts. Our cluttered minds have a direct link to our cluttered lives. Most people have given this little thought or are unaware of the disadvantaged state they place themselves in when they allow negative destructive thoughts to seep into their minds and claim valuable space.

*Negative thoughts linger, guilt condemns, anger suppresses, pain resurfaces, sadness drowns you, fear controls you, insecurity places limits and doubt hinders your progress.*

Your life is captured in moments; reflect on moments that uplift and empower you, these are the thoughts that should occupy your mental space. You have to be aware of the quality of thoughts that live in your space. Take the time to tidy up your mental space. If you would not allow someone to come into your home and destroy your physical space, why would you allow thoughts of fear, guilt, insecurity and doubt to destroy your mental space—your life. Be selective about what occupies your mind.

# GARBAGEOUT

Mental clutter quickly turns into mental garbage causing you to: feel overwhelmed, lose focus, waste your talents and gift and miss out on finding purpose and meaning in life. In the mist of all of this, you lose yourself. Everything is compiling over time and if you are not living in an awareness state, these thoughts take over your mind without you realizing it. These thoughts clutter your mind, shift your focus to a past you cannot change, distract you from living in the present. These thoughts also tell you that there is no use in setting any future goals, which leads to a lack of motivation to take steps to achieve your goals. This is characteristic of a mind that is holding on instead of letting go.

Letting go results in a clear and organized mental space, resulting in clarity about your past, present and future. Centering your thoughts on creating positive mental change opens a path for honest self-reflection and the clarity to move forward with confidence.

Negative thoughts will come, but the faster you shut them down, the more time you will have to spend building skills that will empower you, cultivating qualities that will help you thrive and developing your talents and gift. This is time well spent. Do not waste time on "woulda, coulda, shoulda." Get beyond the cycle of controlling, nonproductive thinking. Today is a new day; seize it and make it great.

Build from within to create mental strength to remain focused despite distractions, make wise choices and be conscious of what you think and what occupies your mind. As you build your mental strength you are gaining control of your temperament, emotions and thoughts; most importantly you are gaining control of your life. As you rid your life of mental garbage, distressing situations will alert you to the importance of staying present, following through, finding a solution and acting with intention. Be determined to grow mentally stronger with each passing day. Free up space, clear your mind of toxic thoughts. Focus on thoughts that will empower you, bring out the best in you; shifting your focus will help you to clearly see your vision, effectively prioritize your life, see your true worth and accomplish your goals.

If you are just letting life happen, your thoughts will be all over the place. Life requires that you be a participant; map out a life plan of your goals. How are you going to achieve your goals? What tools will you need? What will you do if you hit a roadblock? Review your life options. Mapping a life plan will allow you to create a clear vision both mentally and physically; you will be putting yourself in a position to succeed.

Remember who's in control: you are in control of your life, your life is not in control of you, make room to create the space you need to grow. Let go!

*Create a Life Plan*

What do you want to accomplish in the next year, next five years?

_____

_____

_____

_____

_____

_____

_____

Why is it important to be selective about the thoughts that occupy your mind?

_____

_____

_____

_____

_____

_____

What self-defeating thoughts will you let go of today? What will be the benefit?

_____

_____

_____

_____

_____

_____

## IT IS YOUR THINKING THAT SETS LIMITS

That's Impossible
I can't do that
I don't know how

What feelings do these thoughts create: Doubt, Fear and Insecurity

### Think Without Limits

That's possible
I can do that
I can learn

What feelings do these thoughts create: Confidence, Courage, Boldness and Fearlessness

How you think changes the whole mood of your life. Read the thoughts that set limits again then read the thoughts without limits you can feel the shift in your spirit from low to high just from reading these words. Imagine what would happen if you choose to think without limits.

What you THINK you will live and what you LIVE you will BE. Remember that!

Take a look at our YouTube channel TLB TV

**THINK.LIVE.BE**

## BE CURIOUS

When children are curious about something they seek to find answers to their questions. These answers give them the knowledge to grow and develop. A child's curiosity grows even stronger when they are really interested in something. They don't just ask one question; they ask question after question after question until they get a satisfying answer.

Sometimes you lose your curiosity as an adult because of all the distractions surrounding you in your life or you are too afraid to ask a "silly" question. You have to rekindle your curiosity meter. When you begin to ask questions, you find out there really wasn't anything to fear. You find the answers you need to move forward with your life; there is no reason to hold onto fear, doubt or any insecurity about asking questions. You get the opportunity to learn the truth when you ask questions; with each answer you uncover you will grow and develop the courage to continue seeking your truth. So, be curious, ask questions after question after question!

What is something you are curious about?

_____

_____

_____

_____

_____

Are you curious about starting your own business, another career field, strategies to get out of debt, how to have a happy family life, etc.

What questions would you ask if you had the opportunity to find the answers you are seeking?

_____

_____

_____

_____

_____

_____

_____

# GARBAGEOUT

## WRITE FOR YOUR LIFE

Writing opens, refreshes and cleanses your heart and mind
Write about plans now and in the future
Write about your day
Whether negative or positive, sad or happy, frustrated or content, disappointed or relieved
Focus on the positive no matter how hard it maybe sometimes
Learn from the negative—what will I do differently next time to get a better outcome
Control my anger—think, is it worth it, put it on paper, take a deep breath
Pray, sort it out, what made me so upset
Is it really worth getting upset over—the only person you can control is yourself
Practice to get it right, just never give up
Write about happy times and joyous times
Disappointments, setbacks, good experiences, bad experiences
Knowing that brighter days are coming
Strive for success in all that you do—it will come
Success in your family life, Success in school and work
Success in being the best person you can be
Write it down; let it out—then follow your plan to live a happy, meaningful and purposeful life

~ P. Ashworth

## BE COURAGEOUS, BE BOLD, BE FEARLESS

Courage, boldness and fearlessness work harmoniously together revealing your strength, your power and your will to persevere.

***Courage moves you beyond fear, boldness makes you an unstoppable force and fearlessness empowers you to break through the barrier and keep pushing***

When you commit to letting go of fear, doubt and insecurity, you create the space for courage to surface, boldness to emerge and fearlessness to take control. You will develop a new outlook on life, changing your view forever.

What do you want? At work, in relationships and in life, do not allow your life to be suppressed. All the old norms that you hold onto—old thoughts patterns, behaviors and actions—create barriers between you and your success.

In the book, "Lean In," author, Sheryl Sandberg encourages women to *Lean In.* It is the garbage that women hold onto that prevents them from leaning in.

Thoughts of not being good enough, educated enough or talented enough, blinds them from the truth that they are more than enough—their talents usually exceed their counterparts. Women are thinkers, innovators, businesses owners, heads of households and so much more.

This is the time for change in your thinking. Time to be courageous, bold, and fearless; to ask for what we want at work, such as a higher a salary, flexible work schedule—with technology, these things are more possible than ever before. When you take on more responsibility at work expect to be fairly compensated, know the value you bring to the table. Do you want the opportunity to share your ideas? "Raise your hand and keep it up," as Sheryl Sandberg would say, "Then, speak up."

*In work and life, look for ways to create opportunity and ask questions to get you where you want to go.*

So, how do you go about doing this? You change and transform your mind to think in a different way and let go of thoughts that you are inferior because you are not. Mentally, you are just as powerful as the next person.

### No one can make you feel inferior without your consent

It's not who you are that holds you back, it's who you think you are not. Know that you have what it takes to accomplish whatever you want in life. Ask for what you want and be ready to receive. Now is the time to take your life seriously and act in harmony with what you want in both your personal and professional life. When you act with intention, you move your fears, doubts and insecurities from your path.

Act with courage to overcome your fears.

Act with boldness to quiet your doubts.

Act with fearlessness to lift yourself above your insecurities.

Act to hit your target dead center—bullseye!

Ask yourself what do I want out of life?

Once you discover what you truly want out of life; be courageous, bold and fearless in making it happen!

P. ASHWORTH

IF YOU HEAR A VOICE WITHIN YOU SAY, "YOU
CANNOT PAINT," THEN BY ALL MEANS PAINT,
AND THAT VOICE WILL BE SILENCED

~Van Gogh

GARBAGEOUT

## CHANGE IS A PART OF LIFE

You are constantly changing. The world around you is changing, when you look at nature, you see the changes between seasons in weather patterns. Changes happen from one moment to the next.

Look at change as a way to discover more about yourself

Look at change as growth

Change moves you closer to your truth

Change—Think better, Live better, Be better

Our goal in life is not to stay the same, but to learn, grow, change and transform. As you begin to see change as a good thing, your acceptance of self starts to grow. As your acceptance starts to grow, you are accepting yourself and all that you were meant to be. You are no longer hiding, but you are uncovering your truth through acceptance, change—let your transformation take place.

Your attitude shapes the way you experience life. Go with it, enjoy the journey, learn new things, overcome challenges along the way, share your experiences, help others, and most importantly discover you.

What frightens most people about change is change itself. People are fearful of the unknown. Being in your comfort zone makes you feel safe. Things are familiar to you. Change requires that you move beyond your comfort zone into a new environment. Most people settle for the life they have always known. When change is in progress, most people stop too soon, failing to push past the awkward stage of unfamiliarity. Just the thought of being in a strange place keeps most from venturing out, experiencing new things and moving forward. Change can transform your life.

Are you accepting change in your life? Why or Why Not? Give an example.

_____

_____

_____

_____

_____

_____

_____

_____

_____

_____

_____

_____

Do you see change as a good thing or is it a constant struggle? Why?

_____

_____

_____

_____

_____

How can change be beneficial to you?

_____

_____

_____

_____

_____

_____

_Your Outlook Matters_

## BE FEARLESS

Fear will manipulate you into thinking you can't. When your talents and abilities say you can, fear will stop you dead in your tracks, overshadowing your true worth, breaking your confidence to stand up and take action. That's why it is so important to reach a point in your life where fear is no longer an obstacle.

Many people fear what other people will think, potential failure, but you want to learn from failure. When something doesn't work out as planned, find a better way. Never quit, continue to fearlessly move toward your goals. To be fearless means to take chances, be bold, be courageous and move forward with confidence.

### I had fears when creating "GarbageOut"

*Fear of the unknown*

*Fear of going off the beaten path*

*Fear of going where I had never gone before*

*Fear that people would not understand the message I wanted to share, I told myself I would keep sharing until they understood. I am determined not to give up and you should be too.*

When you start focusing more on the specific steps you are going to take to live a life of meaning and purpose, the fear starts to take a back seat because you are not listening to fear, you are controlling the conversation; you are not looking at fear, you are quieting the voice of fear so that it no longer has control over you.

Choosing to live your life in fear of what the future holds breeds worry, dread, apprehension, panic and anxiety. Fear blocks you from finding your passion, using your gift and accomplishing your goals. It starts a domino effect that leads to missed opportunities and unrealized dreams.

Choose to live life fearlessly, believe in yourself, your ideas, welcome new experiences, take risk, let challenges inspire you! Do not be afraid to live beyond self imposed boundaries, knock them down! Choose to truly live life and the only way to live is to release the shackles of fear!

*Change your reaction to fear, see fear for what it is*
*It can be tamed; you hold the power*

To maintain your control, you have to be ready to take on fear.

**Being fearless requires preparation:**

1. Sharpen your focus by writing down your goals

2. Heighten your awareness, list specific steps you are going to take to accomplish your goals

3. Plan for potential obstacles by making an alternative plan

4. Write down your fears, think about the worst thing that could happen then let it go

5. Envision your success and keep it before you at all times

6. Despite feelings of fear take the needed action to bring your goals to life

When you are prepared, your confidence will shine through; although you may feel the fear, continue to take the necessary steps to accomplish your goals, with each step you are fearlessly taking on life. You are being released from the bondage of fear. When you know your strength, your worth; you cannot be intimidated by fear because you have stepped into the present and embraced your power to be fearless.

What do you fear?

_____

_____

_____

_____

_____

How will you tame your fears?

_____

_____

_____

_____

## PUT WORDS TO YOUR VISION

Putting words to your vision begins the process of moving it from an idea to a reality. When your ideas, your vision becomes real to you; you are driven to take action, your vision begins to unfold. You become an active participant in your life, one who takes intentional steps to achieve your desired results. It is so important to keep a journal because as you begin to write down your thoughts about your past, present and future plans, you bring your vision into focus, it becomes clearer and your reality begins to take shape.

Think about the vision you have for your life? Write it down

_____

_____

_____

_____

_____

_____

## BUILDING YOUR HOME, YOUR LIFE

*"I have learned to be self-sufficient regardless of my circumstances, I know how to be low on provisions and how to have an abundance. In everything and in all circumstances I have learned the secret of both how to be full and how to hunger, both how to have an abundance and how to do without, for all things I have the strength through the one who gives me power."* ~Philippians 4: 11-13

Be grateful for the life you have been given. Keep the things you are thankful for in the forefront of your mind. In any given moment in life, your world could change. The shifts you go through in life should not diminish your appreciation for life nor your ability to thrive. No matter where you are in life, there is always a reason to be thankful. This has nothing to do with money, but it has to do with the appreciation for life itself.

### Do You Appreciate Life

You were not promised riches, but you were promised the basic necessities to sustain your life. You have been given a foundation to build your life. Build with fire resistant material so when fear tries to creep in; it does not tear you down. You have to do the work to build a life of fortitude and success.

Just as a house has a designer and builder, you have to design and build your life. You have to pay attention to the details. The appreciation you have for life will determine the type of house you build. Are you going to build a life that is easily broken or torn down? Or, are you going to build a life that is unshakable, one that can withstand the storm?

Assess your needs. What tools will you need? What's your skill set? It takes talent to build a home so you will need to get training or additional help to complete your home.

Regular maintenance is required to maintain a home. A home has to be protected from outside elements, such as the changes in seasons and even invasions. You want to build a home that you will be proud of. The same is true when it comes to building your life. Assess your needs and start building a life that will withstand the test of the elements and come out standing more confident than ever.

What areas in your life do you need help in order to build the life you want to live?

_____

_____

_____

_____

What tools/skills will you need to start creating a meaningful and purposeful life?

_____

_____

_____

_____

What materials are you going to use to build your life? Think about qualities and traits

_____

_____

_____

_____

_____

Cultivating courage, boldness, fearlessness and faith will be a good start.

Take one by one and explain why these materials are important in building your life?

_____

_____

_____

_____

_____

_____

_____

If your home, your life comes crashing down despite all your efforts to build a strong secure life, what will you do?

Will fear overtake you, depression set in or will you be strong enough to start rebuilding again

_____

_____

_____

_____

_____

How can you prepare yourself for the unexpected? Job loss, family emergency, sickness, etc.

_____

_____

_____

_____

*Always be thankful that you have a life that you can build and rebuild if necessary*

## THE OPENING OF CLOSED DOORS

The recognition of who you are becomes so strong when you choose to standup to fear. You walk with courage and strength, confidently knocking down barriers that try to get in your way and prevent you from finding room to grow. You look fear dead in the eye and say, "You have no hold on me."

You have done your research, planned and you are confident in all that you have to give. No one can take this moment away from you. You see the opportunity and you will not let it pass you by. You are clear and confident about what you want and who you are. The cloud has lifted and you see your vision clearly, it is calling you to walk through those doors. Doors once closed have now opened for you. What are you going to do?

Get excited about life! The next chapter is waiting to be lived. Everyday is an opportunity to move closer to discovering your truth. Know your desired destination; when you don't have a vision for your life, goals—you are wandering; you are lost. Have a target to reach.

When your goals become real to you, you are given a burst of energy. You become fruitful; you feel overjoyed. Doors begin to open. Your life is taking root. You know where you are going. Your branches begin to grow, doors open to unlimited possibilities. There will be challenges you have to overcome, roadblocks to knockdown, stand your ground and do not give up.

**Repeat these words: I will, I can, I am determined**

Let go of anything that does not bring value to you and creates a barrier between you and your success. Do the work and open the door to a happier more successful you.

## REFLECT, CLAIM, REJOICE
## YOUR TIME HAS COME

REFLECT ON THE PATH YOU HAVE TRAVELED TO GET HERE. You endured when you saw no way out. When you found the strength to stop looking at the storm, you searched for the door that was patiently waiting for you to walk through. The door was sealed, covered with debris. You started moving one piece at a time until your path was clear. Reflect on the past, take away the lesson and walk on through.

CLAIM THE VICTORY FOR YOUR HARD WORK. Claim what is rightfully yours and do not look back. You have pursued your freedom and stayed the course. You let go of fear, doubt and insecurity to focus on the road ahead. The victory is yours. You have done the work. You have uncovered your truth. Walk through those doors and claim your victory. You deserve it!

REJOICE THAT YOU HAVE PERSEVERED AND ENDURED TO THE END. This is really the beginning, the beginning of the life you always knew. You let go of the thoughts that were trying to defeat you and overwhelm you with fear. You proceeded with courage and boldness to the end. Fearlessness guided your way. Now the doors have been opened just for you. Enter and rejoice because you persevered and endured to the end.

YOUR TIME HAS COME. How will you respond?

**"Expectation postponed makes the heart sick"**
**Proverbs 13:12**

Commit to taking bold, courageous, fearless steps to find your way, to live your truth—your life.

## THE LIFE YOU LIVE IS UP TO YOU

Why remain hidden by fears, doubts and insecurities? Why settle for less than you are worth? Why pretend to be happy and carefree when you are dying on the inside to be free? Let go and be free, free to speak up, be heard and free to just be you.

You hold the key to your freedom—Clear your life of the garbage that has piled up over the years and open the door, walk through. When are you going to get serious about living your life—today, tomorrow, next week, next month, next year?

*THERE'S AN APPOINTED TIME FOR EVERYTHING*
Ecclesiastes 3:1

Now's the Time to Clean House—Get the GarbageOut!

**Let Go and Receive Your Gift**
**The Gift of Freedom**

Look forward to hearing your story
www.garbageoutdaily.com/shareyourstory

*To learn more about the author visit
www.garbageoutdaily.com/aboutus*